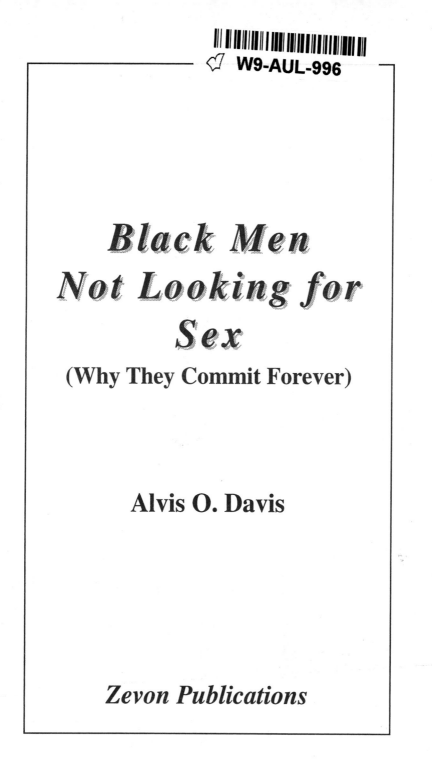

Black Men Not Looking for Sex

(Why They Commit Forever)

Alvis O. Davis

Zevon Publications

Zevon Publications
P.O. Box 4764
San Jose, CA 95150

First Edition
Edited by Carletta Cooley and Robin Merritt
Special thanks to Paul Weisser, Ph.D.

Library of Congress Cataloging-in-Publication
Davis, Alvis O.
Black Men Not Looking for Sex/Alvis O. Davis
ISBN 0-9627656-4-3   94-061196
                                                        CIP

A very special thanks to:

Ralph Brown
Bill Bryant
Deborah Campbell
Lisa Davis
Karl Dumas
Joy Gibson
Gillian Hooper
Larry & Caroline Hughes
Zack Johnson
Constance Jones
Pamala Kelly
Harry & Kasie Nizamian
Michelle Norris
Jerome Rodgers
Cassandra Spellman
Brian & Angie Williams
Geneva Wright

Contents

Introduction

Influenced by an innate desire to nurture, black women play an essential role in helping to maintain loving family relationships.

Commitment is a necessary ingredient that enhances and promotes this nurturing. When black women are loved and respected by their men, the entire black community can be uplifted and revitalized.

This book was written because the strength and well-being of the African American community, as with other communities, is based on the strength and well-being of family. Certainly, stronger black male-female commitment in relationships will mean stronger black families.

Therefore, I do not hesitate to put the group's need for commitment before the individual needs of certain black men "to get over." Nor am I reluctant to suggest to black women unorthodox methods and unconventional wisdom that help to ensure that they get commitment from black men—and get it forever.

Despite everything that black women know and learn, and despite their successes, rarely are they taught how to communicate to black men so that they can get commitment forever. Thus, black women have had a difficult time indeed with black men. Yet, there is no reason why black women should not know what makes black men commit forever. With this knowledge, they will be able to get commitment for the good of their relationship, and thus for the good of the family.

It is a myth that successful marriages come naturally and effortlessly. Researchers have found that nothing could be further from the truth. It takes work!

Still, this is not a "Black Women Have to Do All the Work in a Relationship" book. Certainly, black men must do their part, too. In fact, this is an "If You Are Going to Do Anything to Get Commitment and to Have a Successful Relationship, You Might As Well Do What's Effective" book.

In reality, there are no perfect relationships, but there are *good* ones. If you have ever made mistakes that caused you to lose your man or not get love and commitment from him, this book will reveal to you how to avoid such mistakes in the future.

And although this book is written for your enjoyment, you may not like certain sections. But read on anyway. I am a firm believer that if you have this book in your hands, it is not by accident.

For those of you who are willing to face the reality of your past, present, and future relationships and make any necessary changes, getting a black man to commit forever lies within these pages.

PART ONE

❄

Ensuring
Commitment
Forever

CHAPTER 1

❄

Sound the Alarm

Black men are better lovers and you should beware! While on the surface it may appear positive for black men to be thought of as better lovers, deeper reflections uncover very negative and damaging effects that are associated with how black men relate to their sexuality; so much so that the African American Community, and particularly black women, at least until now, are paying a very dear price. After reading this book, you might want to reconsider how you communicate to your man—or *any* black man with whom you are intimately involved.

In recent American history, not only has black male sexuality been exalted, but black men accept, believe in, and try to live up to the image declared by the exaltation. Even when a black man defines his sexuality as an individual, society still implicates him by race and gender. Invariably, when black male sexuality is portrayed in the media, the portrayal is made to appear as either threatening or enviable.

A majority of the "black movies" of the early seventies, such as *The Mack*, *Super Fly*, *Shaft*, *Sweet Back*, and many others, focused on black male sexuality. Those films helped to negatively define black male sexuality by portraying negative images of how the black man represented himself. Black men throughout the country have emulated what they saw in those films—the actors, style of dress, language, and behavior. For the most part, the films exalted black male sexuality and deflated black female sexuality. Certainly, they influenced the way black men related to black women. To some extent, the worst impact can be seen when we consider those black women who choose prostitution and those black men who choose pimping as acceptable and desirable careers.

The films portrayed the black man's sexuality as his calling card to the world, but especially to women, and as an indication of his strength and power. He might use it to intimately solve his problems or change his world, for which he was often viewed as a hero. Shaft, for example, was the black private detective who was characterized as a sex-machine to all the "chicks."

The trend never stopped. Turn on your television or go to the movies and you will see sexuality still being portrayed as an intricate part of who the black man is. He is likely to rely on it in lieu of intellect or real power. Surely, in dealing with women, his sexuality is often his panacea.

After the popular television miniseries *Roots*, the word *mandingo* became a code word to describe the authority and power of black male sexuality—a description with which few black men had a problem readily identifying because they interpreted it positively.

Even songs, from love ballads to rap, send messages that exalt black male sexuality. Ethnic jokes have in the past reflected, and continue to perpetuate, the idea of the power and superiority of the black man's sexuality.

You may have noticed that, aside from crime, drugs, and unemployment, sex and sports are readily associated with black men. This is all too evident when men from other races automatically assume that if you are a black male, you want to hear what they have to say about women and sports. Many times I have stood in a line at the grocery store and the male clerk or some man in line would start to talk about some sporting event that took place the night before—as if I had sponsored it. On several occasions, men who noticed scantily dressed or well-developed women walking by would proceed to nudge me or smile for my "black male approval." In a few cases, they would simply start to talk about the things they would like to do to her sexually, automatically assuming that their conversation met with my approval and that it could not possibly be against my moral values. After all, I am black and male, and such conversations go with the image as those men understand it. In fact, it is in part the black male sexual image and the black man's attempt to live up to it that make it easier for Americans of all ethnicities to believe that black men are superior in sex and sports, but not necessarily in professional or intellectual endeavors.

The fact that the black male sexual image is continuously exalted, albeit sometimes in strange and twisted ways, has a great deal to do with why black men consciously and unconsciously define their manhood by their sexuality.

Although most black men tend to associate sexuality with manhood, there are those who can establish a more meaningful identity for themselves. These black men realize how unhealthy and counterproductive it is for black men to define themselves by the image of black male sexuality.

How black men evaluate their sexuality, as it relates to their manhood, does not necessarily question whether, but to what degree, they are men. Moreover, their sexual socialization not only affects what they think about their manhood but it heavily influences the way they behave and communicate with black women. For example, the greater lover a black man thinks he is (and the more women he can get to confirm it) not only proves he has lived up to what is often seen as a significant part of the black male sexual image, but gives him permission to think of himself as more than an average man—he becomes a "bad dude."

Even if one does not really know his sexual capability, it is not unusual for an individual black male to identify and define his sexual ability according to his understanding of the collective black male sexual image. Thus, when black men define their sexuality, they usually have the underlying belief that they are better lovers than men of other races. Whether or not they *are* better lovers is not the issue here. What I am addressing is what they *believe* about their sexuality and how these beliefs affect black women and the entire African-American community.

The black man's belief in the power of his penis is often reflected in his attitude. For example, when a black man feels he needs more control over a woman or wants to change her behavior, it is not uncommon to hear him say things like, "If I could only get some [sex], I can make her act right," or "She has been getting out of hand lately—I have to take her home and tighten her up." Or he might insist, "I know what you need" or "You don't know what you're missing!"

Intoxicated by their sexuality, some black men even believe that there is enough power in their penis to make white men pay for slavery by going to bed with white women. Ironically, it is due—at least in part—to the black man's sexual image that white America has tried to forbid relationships between black men and white women.

There are far too many black men trying to live up to what they feel is an expression of black male sexuality. Acting out this sexuality often obstructs, if not ruins, their sense of discipline and their motivation to do anything else. Consequently, many black men seem obsessed with sex. It is as if everything they do and say is for the purpose of taking a woman to bed, while other areas of their lives become secondary, suffer, or completely fall apart. Many of these men actually waste away a lifetime in pursuit of women and sex. They choose their clothes, cars, and even the place they live with that one goal in mind. In the process of womanizing, many black men demonstrate brilliant, creative minds. If this intellect, confidence, and energy used to pursue women and sex were focused toward education, business, and the betterment of black people, the social and economic structure of black society could change in short order. Obstacles would not stop black men. Surely, hearing "no" would not stop them. They would simply have to pursue economic success in the same fashion that they pursue sex.

If you were to give it serious thought, how many black men do you know who actually choose to practice abstinence? I would suspect not many. Abstinence is not a part of the collective black male's sexual image. Therefore, seldom do you see individual black men subscribe to it. Consequently, when you come across one of the few who do, it is surprising, if not unbelievable. As a matter of fact, black men who do practice abstinence are regarded as "abnormal," "square," or even weird.

Perhaps more than any other factor, it is black men's understanding of the black male sexual image and how it relates to their own that causes them to disrespect or betray their relationship with black women. Moreover, because this image suggests that variety in women is the spice of life for black men, the practice of infidelity, heartbreak, and coldheartedness is just fine, so long as the men are "cool" about it. Sadly enough, the black male sexual image often incorporates the idea of making babies and walking away. This problematic influence of the black male sexual image on some black men is so ingrained that nothing less than professional help can bring about change.

Unfortunately, as the negative side of the black male sexual image continues to manifest its ugly head, so does antisocial behavior. Yet, while black women are the primary victims of this behavior, they also have more power than anyone else to stop it. First, they can do many of the things I will suggest in this book to help themselves and their black men. Second, and perhaps more important, because black women have a great deal of influence on black boys, they can play a key role in countering this image of black male sexuality that bombards black boys as they reach adolescence.

Black boys need to be taught certain things about how to respect their own sexuality and the sexuality of black women. All you have to do is look around to see the high number of black women who have babies out of wedlock, frequently without the father by their side. It is not difficult to find black women who are bitter, hurt, and resentful as a result of their relationships with black men who were not taught positive things about their sexuality and how to respect black women or themselves.

Black women must not hesitate to teach and *re*teach

black boys about the harm and pain that the careless, indiscriminate use of their penises can cause not just to females but to themselves. Black boys must be taught more than the perils of making babies and creating financial hardship. Parents must sit down with their sons and explain the lifelong emotional damage created by the "love them and leave them" or "get another notch in your belt" type of thinking that black boys typically grow up with. It is important to emphasize that neither schools nor any sex education programs can be depended on to teach young black men about the negative effects of the black male sexual image.

It is fathers, mothers, brothers, sisters, and all other responsible family members who must teach black boys in their family to respect and morally value their sexuality. If not, the dominating influence of the media will teach them its negative message.

Black boys must understand that when they participate in indiscriminate sex they violate their own bodies. They must learn to resist sexual urges, and say no, just as young ladies are encouraged to do. Furthermore, they should realize that they can be considered whores just like anyone else. Black boys should be clear about the fact that black females will often interpret a sexual encounter to mean more than a casual relationship. For them, it usually involves emotions and means commitment.

In the past, black boys have not been told, and

therefore need to be aware, that this society—including black men—will do a great deal to get them to disrespect their own sexuality, and ultimately black women. They should be taught to feel a sense of connection to the family so that if they start to disrespect any woman, they will feel as if they are also disrespecting their mothers, grandmothers, and all the other women of their family.

American society offers so many negative messages that providing black boys with a healthy understanding of their sexuality is a job that cannot be taken lightly. One should not expect a young man to get a complete under-standing in one sitting. The message has to be gently reinforced to counter the many negative and dominating messages from society. If black boys are not taught a higher understanding of their sexuality, they will grow up and do to women the things you despise.

It is because of past experiences with ill-taught black men that many black women go into relationships with negative attitudes, expecting the worst. Black women everywhere are responding to black men with anguish, defiance, and disappointment. Some develop and fight back with games of their own. Then, if they lose, they scream "foul play."

Furthermore, it seems that anytime the black relation-ship issue is discussed between black men and women, a great deal of finger-pointing takes place. There is no doubt that we can find fault on both sides and much validity to the charges. But instead of arriving at real solutions, the debates usually become arguments about to what degree one is right and the other is wrong. Granted, too many black men don't know how to appreciate a good black woman. But finger-pointing, anger, and resentment do not change the man or help the woman.

Many black women are unaware of the role they play in perpetuating the image of black male sexuality. When they tell black men how much they liked a sexual encounter with them, they exalt their sexuality. In addition, when a black woman acts as if she is controlled by a black man's penis and can't live without it, she helps to perpetuate the image of black male sexuality and his relationship to it. This is not to say that a woman should not show her appreciation or compliment her man. If you feel that he needs encouragement, by all means give it. Positive feedback is highly recommended. But be careful not to overdo it and support a sexual image that can cause both partners problems later. If, for example, he should end up with an overly inflated ego concerning his sexual capability, he might begin to act as if his authority in the relationship should be increased accordingly. Furthermore, his sexual arrogance may encourage unfaithfulness.

Sound the alarm! The truth is, when you communicate to any black man that you would like mutual commitment, you must seriously consider how he has been affected by the black male sexual image. In reality, much of what he has learned is ultimately "anti–black woman" in nature. For many black women, their past relationships stand as proof. It is due in large part to the black man's understanding of his sexuality that black men and women are not the friends they could and should be.

In many cases, when you are with a black man you are interested in, you would be well advised to think of him as an adversary, even if you have known him for a while. Consistently friendly smiles, warm and gentle hugs, flowers twice a week, and access to his credit card do not necessarily mean your relationship is strong enough for him to give you commitment forever.

By thinking of him as a "friendly adversary" rather than as a friend, you are more likely to stay alert until real friendship and marriage bring you together with commitment forever. The advice in this book considers the black male's sexual orientation and tells you how to operate one level above it until you achieve quality commitment that will last a lifetime.

CHAPTER 2

❄

Black Men Not Looking for Sex

Despite their sexual socialization, sex is *not* what black men are looking for when they meet and communicate with women. Believing that it is, and not understanding what black men are really looking for, some black women despise black men. This is also the reason why many black women have decreased self-esteem.

One of the biggest myths perpetuated among black women, as well as others, is that black men are looking for sex. Black men themselves will often go to great lengths to get women to believe that they are looking for sex. But even if he's a stranger yelling what he considers compliments from a passing car window, or he's walking his dog and giving you serious eye contact, or he's someone you have been in a relationship with and he's whispering sweet nothings but saying all the right things, or he's buying you dinner for the first time, the myth that black men are looking for sex is just that—a myth.

The fact that black men are not looking for sex is a primary reason why lovemaking is not a successful tool when one is attempting to initiate a quality relationship or commitment forever. In fact, because sex is not what black men are looking for, it is far more likely to help create bitterness and even end a possible friendship than help to create true love and commitment between a black man and woman. Some black women know, and others may have an idea, that relationships often end in bitterness when sex is involved. Few individuals are aware that black men are not even looking for sex in the first place. If you are to be effective in having the type of relationship you desire, you need to know the reality as opposed to the myth.

Much of society gets its understanding of black male sexuality from sexual stereotypes in the media. Ironically, so do many black men themselves. Nevertheless, their reputation precedes them. This portrait upheld by the media often assists in perpetuating the myth and deceptive perception that black men are looking for sex.

Aside from using sex for procreation, black men, like other men, often use and think of sex as a rite of passage to manhood—that is, he does not consider himself a man until he has had sex. Additionally, he perceives sex as a way of validating his manhood, and as an outlet for pleasure. So for those reasons, it is only natural that black men are going to have sexual desires. But, I reiterate, black men are not looking for sex.

Okay, let me make one thing clear that you are probably aware of: black men do "want" sex, and sometimes with persistent, passionate desire. Still, sex is not what black men are looking for when they are considering commitment forever. This is not just a play on words. There is a serious and distinct difference between wanting sex and looking for it—a difference that can help determine the quality and the extent of his commitment to you.

One may wonder, if black men are not looking for sex, why do they seem to dwell on it and act as if they are looking for it? Indeed, many black women feel that black men seem to focus on sex more than do men of other races, and to them this is an indication that black men are looking for it. But it is the black male sexual image that has a great deal to do with why black men tend to focus on sex. Unfortunately, the image does not readily explain why they are *not* looking for it.

Many people, both black and white, agree that black men, more than white men, either focus on sex or appear to focus on sex when communicating with women. The difference in what black men and white men are taught about their sexuality is a perception to be closely examined. Black men learn that they are expected to be sexually superior to men of other races. They are encouraged and expected to rid themselves of their virginity at an early age—if for no other reason than as a means of "becoming a man." Oh yes, men in other races get a similar message, but usually not to the same degree that black men receive it. White men, for example, learn that they can compensate for a lack of sexual focus with money or success. However, the overriding message to black men has consistently been that if they don't have anything else, at least they have their sexual potency to rely on.

Thus, unsurprisingly, I have never met a black man, young or old, who would readily admit that he was not a good lover. Have you? Black men are expected to know how to please a woman right from the beginning of their first sexual encounter or very soon thereafter. So it shouldn't come as any surprise that some black men are subject to fabricate their sexual experiences. Imagine a black man over the age of eighteen admitting that he was sexually inexperienced and that he needed someone to explain how to go about it! In many circles, he would be ridiculed, laughed at, and thought of as inadequate.

The message is clear to black men at an early age. They have to know what to do sexually, and how to do it well. They should also be adept at getting sex, because being able to get sex is as much a part of the black male sexual image as is knowing what to do when you get it.

We must address this issue because the black man's interpretation of his sexual image has resulted in some notable negative effects on black male-female relationships. It is due in part to the black male sexual image that many black men believe in their own personal sexual ability to please a woman. In fact, some black women will tell you that they quite frankly don't want to date an inexperienced black man. The implication is that they expect black men to live up to the black male sexual image. Unfortunately, black women also say that, in many cases, the only good thing they can get from some black men is sex.

On the other hand, black women also report that there are many black men who don't have a clue about how to please a woman sexually. Some black men may even experience performance anxiety trying to live up to the image. It can be a problem for black women when a black man is not a good lover or is simply a bad lover but thinks that he is great. He is often so strongly influenced by what is expected of him according to the black male sexual image that he inherited that his ego gets involved, and he may not be willing to communicate or listen to advice on how to improve. Some would rather believe that if there is a problem in bed, it is the woman's.

For instance, one black woman told me that as a method of foreplay, her man confidently used his knee to stimulate her. She had difficulty admitting to him that she received no pleasure in the act because he had suggested to her that he was such a great lover. Obviously, he needed to be told. But since he was black and male, he probably felt that it was expected of him to know the right things to do; after all, he was supposed to be superior.

Embodied in the black male sexual image is the perception that sex is nothing more than just "a fun thing to do"—a game that requires a man to devise ways to get it. Consequently, black men play that game so much that many black women have learned to do the same thing. The problem is that most of these black women are reacting to what sometimes appears to be the only game in town. But sex as "a fun thing to do" is not an intricate or well-defined part of the black female sexual image as it is of the black male's sexual image. Therefore, when black women play "the game," they often get confused as to whether or not they really want to or even should be playing what amounts to be *his* game. This problem is particularly evident when they find themselves pretending that sex is "just a fun thing to do" with a black man with whom they would like to have a committed and lasting relationship.

Many black women play the sex is "a fun thing to do" game (better known as casual sex), often hoping that the man they are communicating with will come to his senses, see what a good woman she is, and take her more seriously. You will find that in this book there is a better, far more effective way to get a black man to commit.

In any event, you must understand that this "sex is a fun thing to do" aspect of the black male's sexual image is sometimes so deeply ingrained that for many black men, even "good" black men, casual sex has become second nature. They don't even think twice about it. Thus, sex as just "a fun thing to do" has become an addiction for many black men, but it's still *not* what they are looking for when they are considering commitment forever. Sooner or later, many women find that what I'm saying can be a heartbreaking truth.

Clay and Angela, for example, were infatuated with each other when they first met. During the first two months of their relationship, they did not get sexually involved. One of the things Angela liked about Clay was that he was not trying to pressure her into having sex. In fact, Angela admitted that Clay's style (he did not appear to be sex-craved or have sex on the brain, like many of the other black men she had dated in the past) increased her own sexual desire for him. Even so, Clay had been acclimated to his sexuality like most black men, and having sex with Angela was certainly on his mind. What Clay used was simply a more sophisticated approach.

One day in the middle of the third month, they were kissing and the passion increased to a boiling point. Clay was acting as if he were going to stop, but this time Angela didn't want him to. She had started to think that she had known him long enough, and that he had respected her and could be considered a friend. Moreover, he had even talked of marrying her. It was the talk about their getting married that made her want to wait until after marriage for sex. But now the kissing had gotten her hot and aroused, and her thoughts were that this would be the night that they would make love. And they did.

Afterwards, the two of them felt as though they had found deeper love. Clay went among his friends and bragged that he had "struck gold," insisting that it was the best sex he had ever had. Angela was so thrilled that she could not stop thinking about their future together. For the next four weeks, they spent almost all of their nights together. They couldn't leave each other alone. By the end of the fifth week of their sexual involvement, Clay's schedule got a little busier, and he could only see Angela every two or three days during the week. Then his workload increased, and some other things started to happen, and he barely had enough time to see Angela once a week. Finally, their relationship got to the point where Angela felt fortunate if she saw him once or twice a month. She began to get suspicious and felt that Clay was seeing another woman. Finally, she couldn't find Clay at all, and their relationship was over.

The problem was, in part, due to the fact that Angela gave Clay what he wanted, and not what he was looking for. If Clay had been looking for sex—or even, as in this case, "great sex"—he would have stayed with Angela and married her. After all, he insisted to his friends that he had "struck gold." The truth is, when black men commit to a woman, they don't necessarily commit to the one they have had the best sex with.

Most black men are like Clay. They want sex, whether they are cool about it or not. In many cases, their behavior is simply a reflection of their understanding of the black male sexual image. If they were Jewish or American Indian, for example, they might still want sex, but because their male sexual image is different, they would approach it with a different mentality. Usually, if a black man has not committed to you for life, when you give him sex, you are giving him what he wants and not what he is looking for. As you read this book, you will see how to ensure that what he is looking for ultimately is *you*.

In all likelihood, you have either been in Angela's situation or you know someone who has. Many black women have gone through what she went through. It is often not until their heart is broken that they learn that giving sex to a black man may get them some things, but long-term commitment is usually not one of them. Like Angela, many women are duped into establishing is a "sexship," instead of a well-balanced committed relationship. A sexship is what a man establishes when he communicates with a woman primarily to have sex with her. Sometimes black men do whatever it takes to keep a sexship sailing—and no more. One way you know you're in a sexship is that you're having sex with him and he's not committed to you. Because the focus is often on temporary physical gratification, very few sexships progress into long-term, committed, quality relationships. Sexships commonly serve as a vehicle for black men to validate their manhood and to live up to the confines of the image. Beware! Sexships come and go. Most invariably end up sinking, and quite often taking someone's heart down with them.

In addition, for most black men, having sex outside of a committed relationship tends to shift their focus and the nature of the relationship. This is evident by the fact that many black women say that men often change after they have had sex with them. Those sentiments are probably the reason why women used to ask the once popular question, "Will you still respect me in the morning?"

It's not your imagination. Sometimes black men do become less attentive after they have been to bed with you. Black women are often rudely awakened to discover that many black men will do much more for them in pursuit of sex than they will after sex. One young lady expressed these sentiments when she said that she has had men do everything from repairing her car to painting her house before sex. After sex, as she puts it, it becomes difficult to get a man to fix her a cup of tea.

Indeed, if a black man is pursuing you and there are some things about him that you want him to change, you will have a much better chance of getting your wish if you do *not* have sex with him. If you do give in, and sex becomes the center of attention and the main attraction, other facets of what might have been a good relationship will start to suffer primarily because you gave him what he wanted and not what he was looking for.

Many black men interpret having sex as meaning he has won the "game." At the same time, although they might hesitate to say it to you, black men are highly aware that there is more to a relationship than sex. Most black men can get sex. Availability is not the key issue.

Further proof that sex is what they "want" but not

what they are "looking for" can be seen when you realize that what is far more important to a black man is not whether he has sex with you, but how *you* "played the game." Thus, if he thinks you gave him sex too easily, he is very likely to feel that if he were to commit to you forever, some other man might also be able to get it as easily from you. You will find that for many black men this is one of the worst things they can think about you. You can almost assuredly forget real commitment if they think you are too easy.

Because the black man's manhood is closely associated with his sexuality, one of the strongest signs of his manhood is whether or not he can keep his woman sexually satisfied. If she is seeing another man because she is easy or for any other reason, the implication is that he is not living up to the black man's sexual image and that he might not be the man he is expected to be. In his mind, because his sexuality often has special significance, to lose his woman even momentarily to another man is a significant blow to his ego and his manhood. Therefore, when he is playing games and attempting to have sex with you, he is also evaluating the probability of your being unfaithful.

One could peel back the layers and say it's simply a matter of trust. But he's aware that there are men who play games who can get an unsuspecting, trusting, woman to compromise. Therefore, when a man does fall in love and commit to a woman who he thinks might fall prey to another man, he can become relentlessly possessive, consequently putting a strain on the relationship and making it unbearable for her.

Be clear that when a black man takes you through those changes about having sex with you, he is checking you out. He is checking to see how you might handle any man who might approach you if you were his woman. Like it or not, he does it because he is aware that there are black men out there with many different, unusual, and sometimes complicated games. He is aware that those men are more than capable of getting to women who can't handle the exposure or the pressure.

He knows that it will reflect on him very negatively among other black men if you are weak and give to another man what most black men don't hesitate to call "his stuff." He is likely to perceive your unfaithfulness as a piercing reflection not only of your relationship but also of his position within the ranks of men. In effect, he sees it as a breakdown of his manhood. When a black man believes that this possibility could exist, the most he is likely to establish with you is a sexship—one that will sooner or later sink, no matter what you say or do. It's no excuse, but ultimately what he is doing is protecting his fragile ego as it relates to the black male image.

An even greater problem arises, in that one of the most convincing illusions of a sexship is that it creates a false sense of security. Many women start to think that because they have had sex with a black man they also have a sustainable relationship. They may even start to feel a sense of ownership or that they now have more authority and rights to issues in his life. Yet, because of the way black men have been acclimated to their sexuality, sex to them usually means nothing more than that they have had sex with you. Period. Period. And period. What is worse is that while they are thinking this way, unsuspecting women are starting to invest emotions. They start to care for the men and even fall in love. In the end, what they all too often discover is that they didn't even have a good friendship.

The kind of commitment that sexships get from black men is usually short-lived, if they give any commitment at all. When there is commitment, it is usually one way. The woman is committed, but not the man.

Sexships disguised as balanced, substantive relationships cause black women to end up with decreased self-esteem. They start to feel used and think that they are not good enough to get real commitment after a sexship ends. They are lowered into believing that something is wrong with them, when in actuality they are just fine. Although some black women blame the men, deep down they still feel hurt, confused, and incomplete, and lack self-respect.

Many women go through a cycle of new relationships that lead to sexships. Thus, their negative feelings about black men intensify when their relationships keep turning into sexships. They try to find different or nicer men.

Occasionally, they end up with men who like them, but whom they don't necessarily like. Sometimes they resent these men because they are willing to take a woman with low self-esteem! They might even take out their frustration on these men. What they don't realize is that it was the sexships that started the problems in the first place.

A black woman can be confident that how good a woman she is or how good a lover she is will not matter if she establishes a sexship rather than a balanced substantive relationship. That will only get her negative results. There are many black women who can testify to this. Remember Angela's story. Although the man might return, good sex or even being a good woman is absolutely no guarantee that he will give you commitment. Again, when you give him sex and he hasn't committed himself to you, you are giving him what he wants and not what it takes to get lasting commitment.

This is why having sex with a black man is likely to create bitterness before it creates lifelong commitment. When a black woman gives herself to a man, she is indeed likely to take it personally, become more sensitive, and therefore have higher expectations. Black men are not socialized in the same way. They are more likely to be just the opposite. If you don't already know from experience, it won't take long for you to discover that for black men, having sex doesn't have to be personal or have any emotional attachments or expectations. This is a message that many black women have learned and continue to learn the hard way. It's a lesson that causes black women to despise black men. Many of those black women proclaim that they will never date a black man again—and if they do, they do it reluctantly and often with contempt.

The plain truth is that a black man is much more willing to commit to a woman who morally values her body, her sexuality, and her femininity.

Remember the song, "If Loving You Is Wrong, I Don't Want to Be Right"? If that's your attitude, you might be doing more to build a sexship than he is, and you will likely get the results of your creation. Your weakness is likely to be seen as just that.

When Malika met Isaac, she desired to have sex with him after she had dated him a number of times. Instead, she explained to him that she was not about to have sex with him unless it was under the right conditions. For her that meant m-a-r-r-i-a-g-e. She added that she was more interested in the content of his character than the content of his pants.

Black men have been known to refer to women with Malika's attitude as the "wife type" or the "marrying kind." When a black man hears that term, he usually knows that it describes a woman who does not give sex easily and who morally values her body, her sexuality, and usually her femininity as well. Her motto is, "If Loving You Is Wrong, I'm Just Not Gonna Do It."

Of course, the nature of your sexual relationship with

your man is not the sole factor to consider when getting a black man to commit for life. So relax—this is just the beginning. Throughout this book, you will see what black men are really looking for and why they commit forever when they get it.

CHAPTER 3

Same Man
Different Woman

Different women get different love, commitment, and behavior from the same man. Hence, it's no accident when the black man in your life is treating you either better or worse than other women he has dated. The contrast can be striking. Furthermore, it is usually no accident that in the course of your relationship the way he treats you changes.

According to black women, many black men don't hesitate to talk about their past relationships. Furthermore, some women like to know about them because they believe that knowing how he was in past relationships can lend insight to the present relationship. Even so, the problem is that you can't base your understanding of his past relationships with women solely on what he tells you.

Maybe you are aware of that and think this is an obvious point. On the other hand, I suggest that you not be too quick to conclude. Many women are duped, and you could easily be one, when it comes to believing and accepting what men say happened in their past relationships.

I'm not saying that all black men lie, but what I have found is that the other women's side of the story can be somewhat different—and in some cases, *totally* different—from what many black men describe to their current mates.

The fact is, far too many black women accept as truth what black men tell them about their past relationships. They may do this because often there is some truth in what he says—enough, at least, to convince her.

Invariably, many black men make their ex-partner appear to be the culprit. They emphasize her negative traits and suggest that if there was any suffering, he was the one who had to endure it. They represent her as a bad mother, lover, wife, or girlfriend. They minimize their own negative behavior—unless, of course, they think you will surely find out about it, in which case they may admit it but claim they have been rehabilitated.

I am aware of the influence that black men can have on women after telling them about their past relationships. I have talked to and observed black women who dislike, despise, and have no respect for women they know only through the eyes of their men. They have developed feelings based on the man's version of the nature of those relationships. Many black women go so far as to defend their man's position by saying things like: "Oh, she tricked him into getting her pregnant," or "He only stayed there because of the children," or "All she did was buy clothes and waste his money," or "If she hadn't been messing around, he would still be with her." And the list can go on.

I am reminded of a story a young woman named Marline told me about her new man, Stacy. He had been married for nine years, and during that time had one child. When he met Marline, he told her his former wife was not his type—that she was irresponsible, and he had been miserable in their relationship. He went on to say that he only stayed with her as long as he did because of their child. That story may very well have been true. But black men seldom marry women whom they feel are irresponsible and make them miserable, then stay there for nine years because of a child (who by the way was only four), and be without any fault themselves. In all likelihood he had loved his wife, but the nature of their relationship changed, and that change resulted in a loss of love and finally divorce. When I talked to his ex-wife, her position was that they grew apart and that was the deciding factor in ending their relationship. I don't even think she was aware of his excessively negative feelings about her.

Lori tells how she would see Blake's ex-woman Shirley at work, and how they just didn't like each other. Also, Blake was still friendly with Shirley and would give Lori updates on how negative and contrary Shirley was. But then one day, to Lori's surprise, Shirley asked her if they could go to lunch together. She reluctantly accepted.

It didn't take long before Lori discovered that Shirley was nothing like she had been led to believe, and that their attitude and behavior toward each other had been heavily influenced and manipulated by Blake.

One primary reason that black men create such distortions is that stories about their past relationships are usually directly related to their sexuality, and thus their manhood. The fact is, most black men are going to protect their manhood, and to do so, all too often, includes misrepresenting details in stories about their past relationships.

The result is that many black men, honest and seemingly honest, will tell stories about past relationships in a fashion that will affect and influence your perception of who they are. Consequently, you need to be aware of how you might be influenced by their stories.

In order to get a complete picture of how any black man was in his past relationships, you need to hear both sides of the story, and even that may not be enough. In one sense, it doesn't really matter how the man you are involved with related to women in his past—unless he was or is abusive. Of course, that's reason enough to want to know about any man's past relationships. Nevertheless, since the same man will treat different women differently, what is really important is that he loves and respects you.

Ronny, for example, was well known for being a ladies' man, but his sisters noticed that after he started dating Erica, he changed. He was acting different and treating her better than the other women he had dated. His sisters were curious to know if she was the one—the woman with whom he would settle down and marry. When asked, he would smile and give them a look of approval. He knew very well that he wanted to marry Erica, and she was happy with the way he was treating her. Note that Ronny did not go through any transformation. He was still Ronny, the ladies' man. Ronny had always known how to treat a woman with respect. Erica was simply the type of woman who could get him to do it. In actuality, this is what happens to many black men when it appears that they have undergone a change. It's a typical case of "same man, different woman."

It is partly because of black men's loyalty to their sexual image that black women must insist on the type of relationship that will make them happy. Otherwise, black men will treat them in a manner that is consistent with their understanding of the black male sexual image. As I mentioned earlier, that can easily be a relationship that is void of respect for women. This is why I say that black women have a great deal to do with the type of relationship they get from black men, whether or not they want that responsibility. When a woman ensures that she gets the type of relationship she wants, it doesn't mean that the man does not have to do his part. On the contrary, it ensures that he *will*.

You have probably observed a black man, such as

your brother or a male acquaintance, date more than one woman within the same time frame. Or you may be aware of how he treats the woman in his current relationship, compared to how he treated a woman in a past relationship. You probably can recall that he did not treat them the same. The dissimilarities are sometimes subtle, sometimes blatant. In either case, it's the "same man, different woman" syndrome.

Zack was dating both Sabrina and Pat at the same time. I had the pleasure of watching his interaction in both relationships. When he was at Sabrina's, they were like partners in their relationship. If there was something to be cooked, he would help. He might set the table, cook the meal, or do the dishes. They would talk and come to an agreement on what to do for that evening's activities.

It was an entirely different situation when Zack was at Pat's. She would fix all the food, serve it, and clean up. He would simply tell her what that evening's activities would consist of, and she would comply. Given all that Pat did for him, Zack still showed far more respect for Sabrina. In general, he also treated her better. This was another case of "same man, different woman." This whole issue has very little to do with who cooked, cleaned, or decided what activities were best for the evening.

Pat's primary problem was that she did not insist on much respect from Zack. She acted as if doing good things for him and always being agreeable would allow

Zack to see what a good woman she was and cause him to respond accordingly. But that is precisely how a black man can end up giving a good woman a bad relationship. If Zack continues his relationship with Pat, he will gradually lose more and more respect for her, and this will be reflected in their relationship.

There are two ways that the concept of "same man, different woman" can manifest itself. The obvious one involves three people, as with Zack, Sabrina, and Pat. However, the "same man, different woman" syndrome can also involve only two people. If you and your man are having problems or are in a negative relationship, the following advice can improve your situation for the better. By making the choice to be a different woman, you can enhance the quality of your relationship.

Being a different woman doesn't mean changing who you are; it means being effective with what you do in your relationship. For example, let's drop Sabrina out of the scenario, leaving only Zack and Pat. To get Zack to give her love and respect, Pat would not have to change who she is. But she would need to change some of the ways she is relating to him. The suggestions in this book will show you how easy and effective being a different woman can be.

On the other hand, it's just as important that black women be highly aware that there is a time when being a different woman can create a negative situation for them. Let me explain.

From time to time, many black women have serious problems with their men. The relationship was going along just fine, when, seemingly from nowhere, these men start to communicate to them negatively and/or have affairs. Oftentimes these black men had not completely rid themselves of the negative influences of the black male sexual image. It might be that society's messages about the black male sexual image have rekindled its negative side in him, and he acts it out. Such influences can cause some men to do things they had never done before and others to revert back to bad habits they had before their relationship with you.

You might be aware that some black men can't say no to a woman they desire sexually. If that happens to be your man desiring another woman, the only thing that can stop him or get him to say no is his love and respect for you. Although you might think it should, love alone often won't stop him. Reality strongly suggests that even if he loves you, but doesn't respect you enough, he is likely to mess around. One reason is that, for black men, sex and love have absolutely nothing to do with each other. Remember, sex is what they want and not what they are looking for. They have been socialized to engage in sex with no thoughts of love. Hence, they believe they can do it without it having any meaning.

In any event, aside from a relationship with God, it is usually because of their relationship with you that most men change their behavior and cease being influenced by the negative aspects of the black male sexual image. Seldom do they wake up one day and say, "I'm going to start treating black women right, and I'm going to be faithful regardless of all temptation." Unfortunately, that thought is slightly too radical for many of those men who subscribe to today's black male sexual image.

How your man behaves when he is attracted to other women is going to be influenced by the black male sexual image, or you, or both. Therefore, when a black woman finds that she has a man whose behavior has digressed, it's often because her influence has lessened and the influence of the black male sexual image has increased.

A black man is more likely to succeed at bringing a good woman a bad relationship if she forgets that relationships are often in transition, particularly a new one. Maybe more importantly, this can also happen if she forgets that her man, as much as she might love him, is still likely to be influenced by the black male sexual image.

While this does not absolve black men of responsibility, it is reality. Moreover, this whole reversion process often takes place when you are feeling excessive love for him. Sadly enough, that's often because some black women, out of love for their man, or out of a new sense of insecurity, or for whatever reason, change and become more tolerant of his negative and disrespectful behavior. In doing so, they may be acting like a different woman, at least different from the one he had loved and respected.

Thus, seldom is it an accident when he treats you differently from the way he used to. This, too, is a case of "same man, different woman."

Obviously, this "same man, different woman" syndrome is less likely to occur if you are consistent and remain more like the woman he fell in love with and married. You can get and maintain a positive relationship with any black man if you insist on respect and, if necessary, are willing to let him go for lack of it.

But don't worry! The next chapter reveals a simple, easy, and effective method that you can use to recognize and address many relationship problems.

CHAPTER 4

❄

How Do You Rate?

With exceptional consistency, I can tell you why you do or do not have a quality relationship with the black man in your life. I can also consistently predict the likelihood of whether he will ask you to marry him, and then, if he will follow through and make the commitment. Furthermore, it is in this chapter that I will look into your relationship and tell you whether or not he will commit to you forever and what you can do to change things if commitment is not in his plan.

Admittedly, I have no special powers that allow me to glance into your personal relationships. But I can still fairly accurately make those predictions. Better yet, you too can easily and accurately predict the fate of your relationship with the black man in your life. Plus you can have him eating out of your hands if you want. You simply have to understand your love power and project it accordingly.

Let's begin with a 10-point Love Scale (1-2-3-4-5-6-7-8-9-10), with 1 representing "no love," 5 "average love," and 10 "maximum love." Rate your love for the man in your life. If you have a problem with trying to determine how much love you have for him, trust your first thought, because there lies the true answer, and only you can know it. While there is no right or wrong answer, you should not base your response on any one good or bad act. Therefore, your response should not be based on a particularly good time or a disagreement from the day or night before. This rating can be done for any relationship, regardless of how long you have been together. Stop now and rate *your* love for him.

You will be able to use this simple scale to monitor the power of your love as it relates to your relationship. The only adjustment that I want you to make is that if you rated your love for him a 10, change it to 9 for the time being.

Now that you have used the scale to rate how much you love him, we can start to look at the nature of your relationship and make any necessary adjustments. But before that, let's do one more rating. Using the same scale (1-2-3-4-5-6-7-8-9-10), rate *his* love for you. Use the same philosophy as before, trusting your first impression. Don't ask him or anyone else how to answer. This rating is based on how much you *think* he loves you. Similarly, this rating should not be based on any one act, but should represent your overall feeling. If you have not already done so, rate his love for you now.

Now that you have completed the ratings, we can get to the essence of many problems that black women have with black men. First, the reason I asked you to make the maximum rating of your love for him a 9 was to leave room in the event you thought that he had slightly greater love for you. However, if you rated your love for him greater than his love for you, that could be one of the problems, if not the biggest one, in your relationship. A black woman who loves her man more than he loves her has problems with the man, and consequently has problems in the relationships.

This dilemma can be very frustrating for black women who think that it is ludicrous not to allow love to simply flow in a relationship. Furthermore, they think it is the healthy thing to do—particularly if they are married. For many women, allowing love to flow is a natural process, and a man should be secure enough and mature enough to handle it. In addition, many black women have learned that the more love given, the more love returned. If only this were a perfect world!

But to further drive home the point, if you think back on any failed relationship you have had with a black man that ended before you wanted it to, you will find that you loved the man more than he loved you. Moreover, if you think about any female friend who is in a relationship plagued with problems, you will be able to conclude that she, too, loves her man more than he loves her.

The bottom line is that black men don't appear to be able to handle you loving them more than they love you. How much more you love them than they love you may well be a determining factor in (1) whether or not he will ask you to marry him and follow through, and (2) the quality of your relationship afterwards.

The irony is that black men want you to show love for them, and many will go to great lengths to ensure that you do so. They know that the more love they can get you to show and feel for them, the more secure they will feel about the relationship. Many of you realize this and, as a result, go to great lengths to assure your man of how much you love him, even if it has meant proving that you love him more than he loves you. Yet, black men have consistently shown that they aren't able to handle this.

Perhaps when some black men feel you love them less than they love you, they continually feel a need to find ways to increase your love. Perhaps, consciously or unconsciously, they feel that until you obviously love them more than they love you, they have not lived up to the ideals of the black male sexual image. Thus, they must focus their energy and time on you.

On the other hand, it may be that when black men feel you love them more than they love you, their sense of manhood or ego is completely satisfied. The black male sexual image sends a clear message for that kind of superior position. The message is that when he has the upper hand in your relationship, he is complete and it's okay for him to find other women to run his game on and/ or conquer.

Many a black man has ruined a good relationship

because his woman loved him more than he loved her. It can happen within the first month of a new relationship, or ten or twenty years after marriage. The problem for some black men may arise because some women have a tendency to accept less respect when they feel more love for their man than he appears to have for them. But as I mentioned earlier and emphasized in the book *The Cold Reality*, losing your man's respect will cost you happiness as well as your relationship. In fact, regardless of how much you love him, of the three most important things you must have in a relationship with a black man, respect is number one, and the other two are respect and respect—in that order. It's that important. Don't leave home or get involved without it!

But back to the Love Scale. Your ratings say a great deal about the nature of your relationship. They are also a good indication of the power and influence of your love on the relationship. The Love Scale can be used as a focal point. With it in mind, you will be able to make a bad relationship good and a good relationship better. If the Love Scale is properly balanced, a black man will love you more than you love him, and you will be in a position to easily get commitment forever!

If you indicated that your love for each other was about the same, or if you rated him as loving you more than you love him, and that's *truly* the way it is, you have fewer problems with your man than do women who love more. Surely you want to keep it that way. The more love he has for you, the more willing he will be to commit to you—and do so forever.

But there are many black women who were once in your position and are now in negative relationships. Many of them fail to realize that relationships are often in transition. Because relationships change, you should use the Love Scale to monitor and ensure that he continues to love you as much as you love him, and preferably more. As you read further, you may see some of the things that you automatically do with your man that cause him to love you. You will also be able to understand what will certainly make a black man continue to love you as much as you love him, or more.

Women who rate themselves as having more love for their man than he has for them must and can change this unhealthy imbalance in order to get lasting happiness and commitment forever. How and what to do will depend on the size of the gap between the two ratings on the scale. For example, a woman who says that her love for her man is an 8, but his love for her is a 6, has a good chance of changing her relationship so that he will love her as much as she loves him or more, because there is only a 2-point difference.

Keep in mind that the numbers are not exact, but rather an indication of how you feel. A woman who says her love for her man is an 8, but his love for her is a 3, can also change her relationship around for the better. In this situation, there is a 5-point difference. Therefore, she might have to work at it a little more diligently than someone who has a 1- or 2-point difference on the Love Scale. It is also very likely that the woman with the greater point-difference is having more problems in her relationship.

While you can make almost any relationship work, no matter what the difference is on the Love Scale, some of the women who feel there is a 5-point or greater difference may find that the best solution is to back away from the relationship to make it work, if it is going to work at all.

In any event, when your love exceeds his, quite often many of the things you do to show greater love will not mean as much to your man. Furthermore, the greater the gap on the scale, the less those things will mean to him— to the point that even smothering him with love will have little effect or may even turn him off completely.

On the other hand, ironing out differences, going through tough times, and communicating in general are easier when he loves you just as much as you love him, or more.

There are three ways to change the Love Scale so that your man will love you equally or more than you love him. One way is to decrease your love for him. At first, this might sound a little harsh, but when the situation is appropriate, you will find it applies quite well. The idea is not for you to stop loving your man, but for you to stop being the victim of your love for him. Some black women will find this to be a very effective strategy. For example, you might be loving him too much if you do everything you can to please him, but it seems nothing is enough. He doesn't seem to appreciate even the big things and shows very little gratitude or respect. Yet, you continue to do things for him, and he continues to care less. If this goes on, he is bound to lose interest in you. Negative thoughts and communication can easily take over and suffocate such a relationship.

In order for you to realistically have the necessary strength it will take to carry out some of the things that will be suggested here, you may need to decrease your love for your man. You decrease your love by first concentrating on how you compare on the scale. Since how much love you have for him (regardless of your reasons why) is based on a decision *you* made to have that amount of love, now is the time to change that decision. Start by focusing on his not-so-good qualities—the things that you don't really like about him. Focus on those traits long enough until you begin to see yourself go down on the scale. It could happen instantly, but it could also take weeks. You will know you have effectively decreased your love when you no longer want to—and *won't*—do things for him unless he gives you respect and shows genuine gratitude.

Focusing on the not-so-good qualities can cause you to become very dissatisfied and even angry with him. He will sense that you have changed and will probably challenge you. Operating from anger does not make you a balanced person in dealing with him. If you have to be angry to bring changes that lead to increased love from him, you will not be successful. You will be far more effective in reaching your goal the moment you clearly realize that it is the power of your love and not the power of your anger that will create the necessary change. You must, however, focus on his not-so-good qualities, allowing those thoughts to motivate you to use the power of your love properly.

A second way to change the Love Scale in your favor is for you to effectively use what you have to get him to love you more. That, too, is what this book is about. By addressing certain issues, you will see why black men love and commit forever. You will find that it's not so much that you are a good woman, but rather that you are a woman doing the right things. Only then will you begin to see your man love you more and more.

The third method is a combination of the first two: you cause his love to go up while simultaneously lowering yours. In many situations, this approach will be the most effective. The proof will be in your relationship. You will know you have been more effective because he will be touching, holding, and wanting you more than ever. In effect, he will be continuously loving you as much as you love him, or more. He will want to love you and commit to you forever—and that's our goal.

Still, be sure not to make a classic mistake—which

occurs when a woman gets her man to love her at least as much as she loves him, but her response to his increased love causes things to go awry. For example, she might be at a 7 while he's at a 5. By decreasing her love to a 6 and getting him to come up to a 6, she brings balance to the love in their relationship. As he becomes equally or more loving, caring, attentive, and desirous, she recognizes the effects of balanced love in their relationship. Ironically, it is his increased affection that causes her to make the classic mistake of again increasing her love for him. After getting her man to equal her love at 6, she then reacts by loving him even more and returning to 7 or higher, thus creating another imbalance. Remember, the quality of your relationship will invariably depend on keeping your love balanced—or imbalanced in your favor.

Surely there are idealists who will argue that this approach is manipulative, mechanical, or unnatural. To you I say that it is for the good of *both* partners. I am suggesting some of the things that get increased love and commitment from black men. The alternative is all too often less appealing. Therefore, for those individuals who are ready to be a different woman with the same man, I suggest you get started by decreasing your love at least to a level that equals his love for you. But don't stop there. In the next chapter, I will discuss ways that you can use to increase his love.

CHAPTER 5

❄

Compatibility

Many a black man is unaware that what he establishes when dating you is not quality bonding but a weak misguided linkage that seldom holds a relationship together. Then he's subject to leave you because of it. In essence, it is precisely because of what the relationship lacks that it never had a chance. And while the foundation he establishes is mostly an innocent act, it bears unfriendly consequences. Very often the relationship ends after your heart gets involved—or worst yet, after marriage. The problem is compounded when you unwittingly, and often desiringly, go along with this unwholesome relationship.

Compatibility is the necessary footing upon which relationships endure or collapse. It is a primary element that black men look for, want, and need in a relationship. The way black men court women causes them to develop relationships that lack the necessary ingredients for genuine, stable compatibility—particularly the type of equanimity that will help establish a foundation for long-term commitment.

Thus, what you end up with are relationships that cannot endure. They become uninteresting, don't have what it takes to survive, and are susceptible to falling apart during crisis or pressing problems.

After what was seemingly a perfect courtship of two years, Russell and Gloria got married. Now, just four years later, they are talking about getting a divorce. Russell recalls their courtship days as the best time of their relationship. Their first date was a balloon ride over some very romantic California landscape. From that date on, everything appeared to be going fine. They both loved the outdoors. On occasion, Gloria would fix baskets of their favorite foods, and they would go on picnics. They both liked the same type of music, and occasionally Russell would surprise her with tapes of recordings that they treasured. They frequented movies and plays together. Gloria admits that she had never been so romanticized. Russell points out that it was easy to romanticize Gloria because they enjoyed many of the same things. Meanwhile, as they communicated, love flourished between them and they got married. For the moment, let's leave them in their joy and consider another couple, Diane and Gordon.

Diane laments that during the year she and Gordon dated, he didn't romanticize her very much because he was unemployed when they met. They did, however, spend a lot of time at her house watching television and videos, playing board games, and indulging in various other activities that the two of them enjoyed.

The pattern of communication in both relationships is typical of the way black men court black women and the way black women expect to be courted. The men pursued and established their relationships through dates of entertainment. What inevitably happens is that black couples usually base their relationship and the extent of their compatibility on how much the two of them like the same types of entertainment. For example, both Russell and Gloria like the outdoors, picnics, the same types of music, and plays. Diane and Gordon like the same types of movies, television programs, and board games.

At first glance, everything seems just fine. However, a second look at both couples reveals a courting strategy that has inherent problems. It's a courting strategy that men of other cultures also use, but I am addressing black relationships in which this strategy is one of special concern because of the excessive negative effects. Since many black couples establish their relationships through dates of entertainment, entertainment compatibility becomes the foundation upon which their relationship attempts to stand but usually falls.

There is nothing wrong with entertainment compatibility. It's refreshing and a good thing to cultivate in a relationship, but it's not the whole relationship. When couples rely on it as an indication that they have a balanced and wholesome relationship, and then get married because of it, problems are bound to develop.

Couples fail to realize that they can only entertain each other or be entertained for so long. Sometimes it's simply a financial drain to maintain a relationship focused around entertainment compatibility. In any event, quality relationships demand more substance. When a relationship that is developed around entertainment compatibility loses it's luster, it becomes monotonous and uninteresting, and somebody wants out.

Most black men establish relationships around entertainment compatibility because they realize that they will get a good response from women. But then, all too frequently, these same men break the alliance when they come to realize that it is not what they want because the relationship is one-dimensional and lacks other bonding qualities.

Typically, many black men feel less of a need to maintain entertainment compatibility as a relationship matures. It is no coincidence that this is also when the romance seems to slow down or dissolve altogether. For these men, entertainment compatibility is more a strategy used to attract and get a woman than it is a strategy to maintain a relationship.

Many black men will stop being concerned about entertainment compatibility shortly after establishing a sexual relationship with a woman. This is a typical pattern. It is at this point that many black men attempt to shift the nature of the relationship from entertainment compatibility to a sexship. If you recall, a sexship is a relationship centered around sex—one in which the men sometimes do just enough of whatever it takes to keep it going.

Obviously, neither a sexship nor a union that centers around entertainment compatibility has the qualities necessary to maintain a wholesome and balanced relationship. That is why it is not uncommon for a woman in either of these types of relationships with a black man to wonder why he will not give quality commitment, or commit forever. She doesn't realize that, in his mind, the nature of his courtship with her has been reduced to him bouncing between entertainment compatibility and a sexship—which can also be an entertainment compatibility. Most black men will not give quality commitment in this situation because there is nothing particularly special or unique about the relationship. It is one that they can establish with other women, particularly those who have lower standards. But once this kind of relationship is established, many black men will enjoy themselves and have no problem with this type of merger until the woman starts to believe that it is a quality relationship and begins to want quality commitment or commitment forever.

What many black men are looking for during the dating process, but hesitate to admit, is a woman that he desires sexually but has the ability to refocus his energy. This is best accomplished by a woman he has *not* had sex with, although it can be done after becoming intimately involved as well. Since he is interested in her, she has the power to mold him and the relationship into what she desires. Getting commitment at this point is much easier. When sex is introduced to a relationship in which the proper foundation has not been laid, it can become much more difficult to get black men to focus on the commitment women want. After sex, men are often much more influenced by what their black male sexual image says than by what the woman has to say.

When Aleda first started to date Bernard, he took her to her choice of entertainment spots. They soon became sexually involved, and about that time Bernard lost his desire to take her places. They got into a pattern of staying home and having sex. He always had a good reason to avoid taking her out. When she decided that she wanted more from the relationship, he complained about her putting pressure on him. For two and a half years, Bernard had things his way.

Although he didn't get what he was looking for, he got what he wanted: sex and home entertainment—but mainly sex. Thus, there was no need or significant reason for him to establish quality commitment. It is after entertainment compatibility or sexships have been established that misunderstanding and miscommunication take place. Meanwhile, hearts get involved and are intentionally or unintentionally broken. The irony is that sometimes it's not until after marriage that a relationship based on entertainment compatibility and sex loses its fire.

The remedy to this problem is to develop a relationship around common interests—not in lieu of, but preferably along with, commonly enjoyed entertainment. Common interest projects are the things that the two of you have an interest in and do together, but for other than purely entertainment value. For example, if you and he both have an interest in acting and take the time to pursue that endeavor, you have a common interest. Likewise, if the two of you want to open a day-care center and work with children, you have a common interest project. The absolute best common interest you can have is a sincere love for God and a desire to study His Word and serve Him. Nevertheless, if you were to get a man with that kind of interest, he still won't be perfect. In fact, he could be far from perfect, but at least he's trying to enrich his soul and spirit.

The key to a good common interest project is to ensure that it is something that you both truly want to do, and that it is not something that one of you likes doing and the other simply pretends to enjoy and goes along. There is a significant difference between common interest and common entertainment. Common entertainment is something you do simply for its enjoyment value. With common interest there is more purpose, more work—mental, physical, or both. You become more intimately involved in each other's lives. Relationships that have common interest not only stimulate quality communication, but they help to establish bonds that enhance good friendships. Subsequently, common interests also enhance romance.

The more common interests you have, the greater the chance he is going to want quality commitment and to commit to you forever. In contrast, relationships that lack common interests tend to grow apart.

I have heard of couples who made their children such an intricate and prevailing common interest that when the children grew up and left home, the parents were at a loss as to what to do with themselves. There is certainly nothing wrong with having children as a common interest, for it's only proper. On the other hand, seven out of ten black women who bear children find themselves raising them without the father in the home. Children should be a definite common interest, but obviously they are not enough to sustain a quality relationship with most black men. If you think that children are a strong enough common interest to keep a relationship with a black man together, look at the statistics again and remove the thought from your mind!

Be on the alert! Don't let your relationship hide behind entertainment compatibility. It can divert your attention away from developing common interests, which usually takes more discipline. *Discipline* is the key word here.

Indeed, a relationship may be able to get by on nothing more than entertainment compatibility. Usually the more money one has, the more one can rely on common entertainment as a substitute for common interests. You can always ensure that your common entertainment remains invigorating and fresh. Even so, it's still not advisable to build on it alone.

Smartly guide your relationship to areas of common interest. If you find that you can't establish common interests, it's an indication that you are not very compatible. If that is the case and you are already married, as an alternative make sure you have quality entertainment interests.

But when you have both common interests and common entertainment, you have the best of both worlds and the ingredients for a more balanced and quality relationship. This is the foundation on which his love can be built to great heights. His love will almost certainly increase on the Love Scale. Destiny is in the palm of your hands. Mold it with common interests.

CHAPTER 6

※

Two Relationships in One

Disagreements have a tortuous way of invading and assaulting the most wonderfully endearing relationship you can experience. Sometimes a relationship can fall completely apart if you are unaware that you and he have two types of relationships in one. What can be the height of love and romance in one aspect of your relationship can turn into insecurity, anger, and distrust just a few hours later because of the other, more fragile side of your relationship.

Instead of eating strawberries and counting stars as the two of you might have planned earlier, you are exchanging insults while discussing how to divide the furniture. The entire experience, at least for a heart-pouncing moment, may seem as if the more fragile side of your relationship will surely end it all. But if you are fortunate, you will have enough love for each other to endure and carry on.

Meanwhile, the scars that such an encounter leaves behind rip and tear at the edges of your relationship. Should the pattern continue, it might eventually become a primary part of the way you communicate, until it desensitizes the very core of what you are trying to build. In such a situation, obviously your love for each other, and thus your relationship, will begin to deteriorate.

Understanding the two types of relationships you share with your man may shed some light on why one is often more important to him, or why he's usually more sensitive about it. Hence, it will also help keep the more fragile side of your relationship from destroying the entire connection.

When communicating to black men, you would be well advised to know that within your union you have a *private* relationship (the relationship you have with him when there no one else is present) and a *public* relationship (the relationship you have with him when one or more other persons are present). It doesn't matter who the other people are or how well they know you.

Most black women are unaware that they can have an endearing private relationship with their man and at the same time have a public relationship that can turn the entire alliance into a nightmare. Many relationships between black males and black females are destroyed because of the couple's public relationship. Moreover, black couples may have numerous disagreements in their private relationship, unconsciously anticipating and preparing for what may be revealed in their public relationship.

Many of the disputes that black women have with

their men can be avoided once they effectively deal with their public relationship and how it affects their partner. In many cases, he doesn't even realize there is an effect on him.

Among the things that influence his perception of his manhood, his relationship with his woman in public is at the top of the list. As his companion, like it or not, you represent him, sometimes more than he represents himself. Some black men may not say it, but many have no problem telling you quite frankly that they feel you represent them. Don't interpret that to mean only in a formal setting or an environment in which strangers are around. It can mean anytime and anywhere there is a third person (or more) present, regardless of who that person is. It could be your mother or brother, his mother or brother, or a best friend who has known you or him longer than you have known each other. That person is still a third party. Third parties could even be your children, particularly if they are old enough to understand the concept of a relationship.

Not only do black men feel that you represent them in your public relationship, but they perceive that representation as a reflection of their manhood. Thus, the value that some black men place on their manhood often far exceeds their need for a relationship with a woman who does not mind demeaning them publicly.

While men of other ethnic groups also have public and a private relationships with their women, they may not associate these so closely with their manhood or sexuality as black men do. Subsequently, they may have more tolerance in their public relationships than black men do.

With black men, the same disagreement or problem that they may have in a private relationship can escalate into an ugly situation in a public relationship. Black men are far more sensitive in this area than many care to admit. A disagreement, misunderstanding, or any perceived negative act, particularly something that seems embarrassing to a black man, can be much more piercing in your public relationship than if it happened in your private relationship. Not only can problems be more offensive when they surface in your public relationship, but they also tend to persist longer.

In addition, your public relationship is often where the power within your total relationship is displayed. Close examination often reveals the level of commitment that you both have for each other. A black man knows that other people, and particularly other black men, will look at the nature of his public relationship and immediately determine his power and capability to maintain the relationship. The nature of his public relationship with you can also suggest whether or not he is satisfying you sexually. On numerous occasions, I've talked to black men who have watched a man's public relationship and then drawn conclusions about the faithfulness of his woman, taking special note when they believe that she would be unfaithful.

Equally important to black men is the degree of respect other black men will give him, based on his public relationship with his woman.

Most black men will never say to you: "Hey sweetheart, I feel social pressure from black men and people in general when we are in our public relationship. Would you please give them the strong impression that I am the head of this relationship? Because of my ego and my identification with black male sexuality, it would help me to feel like a worthwhile man, and the quality of our relationship would be much better in the long run." Instead, some men attempt to verbally and sometimes physically challenge or beat you into submission in your private relationship so that when you are in your public relationship they can expect fewer problems. Other men use the same tactics when you are around people, and, if necessary, challenge you in both your private and public relationship. Sometimes, when you see loud, argumentative couples, she is unaware that he might be simply trying to establish his position in their public relationship. It probably doesn't matter what the issue is about.

Then there are men who simply avoid their public relationship as much as possible. When this is the case, women often spend a lot of energy trying to get those men to take them places, while the nature of the public relationship could be the hidden reason for the men not wanting to go. It might be that they have either already suffered what they think is a blow to their manhood (ego), or they simply choose not to take the chance. If a woman is too assertive in her public relationship, her man may develop his own public relationship, so that their social lives revolve around two separate worlds—one for him and one for her.

There are black women who sense that their men are less assertive in their public relationships (or just don't care), so they use their public relationship as a venting forum in an attempt to correct problems they have in their private relationship. Typically she waits to talk about him—sometimes in the worst kinds of ways—until one or more other people are present. Often she is telling nothing but the truth. She senses that he does not want his public relationship to be this way, so she tries to embarrass him into changing negative habits and behavior. It is a tactic that seldom if ever works, and it usually causes many more problems than it solves. Not only can it cause some men to stop caring about their public relationship, but this tactic usually affects a couple's private relationship in a negative fashion as well. He surely won't have more love for her in his heart or on the Love Scale.

I recall being at a social gathering in which a game of volley ball was being played. Being overly concerned about the quality of play, a young lady kept screaming in a degrading fashion to her man: "You are weak! You are weak! Can't you do any better!" Ultimately, she only wanted a better performance from him, but she was challenging him at the expense of his ego and their public relationship. Such insensitivity can cause her many problems, if not cost her his love in the long run. Surely, this man will hesitate before he wants to play volley ball with her again.

The key is to remember that men behave differently in private relationships than they do in public ones. In many cases, a black man's public relationship is so important to him that he will leave a woman because of it, and usually without identifying it as the primary problem. It is a major concern for a man when he sees that a woman won't hesitate to disrespect or embarrass him in their public relationship. There are also black men who are so sensitive about their public relationships that when things go awry, they don't say anything for fear that they might lose control and react too irrationally.

On the other hand, there are black men who will take advantage of a woman who simply gives them total control of their public relationship. These men don't hesitate to show others, at her expense, just how much control they have. It is usually an indication that their respect for her is not what it should be.

Harvey was in a bookstore talking to two other male friends. His companion, Yvonne, who had come with him, was waiting patiently. She had told him earlier that she was late for her next appointment and that they should be going. Yet, one could tell from the way she talked to Harvey, and by her body language, that she was giving him respect in their public relationship. Nevertheless, Harvey took the opportunity to demonstrate his power and control and disrespect. Ignoring her need to get to her appointment, he asked her to go to his car and get a document to support a point he was making in a conversation that was virtually insignificant. When she courteously complied, he all but pounded his chest.

It is the type of behavior so often demonstrated by men like Harvey that makes some black women defensive. They get to the point where they could not care less and become insensitive to their public relationship. You can catch them aggressively challenging their man and trying to put him in his place at every opportunity. However, the answer is neither total submission nor overly assertive behavior.

Actually, it is possible to make some men "act right" when they realize you will expose them in your public relationship. But this is a negative form of communication that will eventually get you negative results, and is therefore not advisable.

The public relationship should be a part of a well-balanced union. Therefore, with a little maneuvering, either both of you or you alone can manage it effectively and positively.

You must first accept that it is the presence of other people that influences your public relationship. Third parties can be innocent bystanders who never say a word. They may not even want to have anything to do with the problem(s) in your relationship. That does not matter. Their presence is the only thing that is needed.

Furthermore, if you ask other people for input, you have to see yourself as one who is soliciting unprofessional advice. You have put them in a position of having to give input on your relationship, knowing that they may jeopardize the love and friendship they share with you and/or your man. Although they may mean well, their hearts cannot be involved in the same way yours is, regardless of who they are.

This is not meant to imply that you should ever suffer in silence. Surely, there will be times when you need advice from someone else. The point here is that unless you and your man agree in advance, you should not bring up your problems during your public relationship. You can always get input when he is not there. If you don't like talking about him behind his back, either get his permission or don't worry—he's not likely to find out everything you say about him anyway. Be aware that society in general no longer expects people to work very hard to keep a relationship or marriage going. Your relationship or marriage must be held together from within. The lyrics of a popular song say it best: "Don't ask my neighbor, come to me." Indeed, that is how it should be with you and your man.

Quite often, the more well-bred and cultured a black man is, the more concerned he is about his public relationship. Such a man tends to look for a woman who understands the importance of his public image, thinking of such a woman as "sophisticated."

Nevertheless, you and your man should have an understanding or policy concerning your public relationship. Even when his ego tells him to say it's not necessary, you should warmly persist. Obviously, such a policy can help you avoid many unnecessary problems. Your objective should always be to attempt to uplift each other in your public relationship. The policy does not have to be perfect, and you should not expect perfect results. But here are some suggestions:

1. You should expect some problems with the policy. Otherwise, you are setting the whole process up for failure.

2. The policy should be centered around mutual respect and mutual support. In fact, your thoughts and goals should be to uplift each other at every reasonable opportunity.

3. You can agree to have secret signals in public situations. For example, a pull on the earlobe can mean "I love you." Or scratching the eyebrow can mean "Let's wait and discuss this in private." Or closing one eye can mean "I love you, but you are embarrassing me, so please stop."

4. The key is not to get to the point where you cannot laugh at yourself or realize that sometimes the joke is going to be

on you and it might be a little embarrassing.

5. Finally, if one of you feels that you will be teasing or affronting the other in your public relationship, it would be nice to forewarn the other.

You will find that implementing one, two, or all of the above suggestions can improve your public relationship and thus improve your overall union. Manage your public relationship wisely. Doing so will increase his love for you in both your public and private relationships.

PART TWO

❄

THE
PSYCHOLOGICAL
EDGE

CHAPTER 7

❄

The Hidden Power of Compliments

Drained of the confidence she once had in herself, Dorothy now wonders if she is even worthy of a good man. It seems as though the only thing she is sure of is that Don was going to eventually leave her for someone else. Surely, he would act like the other men in her past. The pattern was clear. At first, they would tell her how great she was, and eventually they would start to criticize her. It was a pattern that invariably had disastrous consequences—so much so that she was starting to dislike herself. Unfortunately, like so many other women in similar situations, Dorothy was becoming her own worst enemy.

Close examination reveals that many women make the same mistake. Perhaps unknowingly and therefore unintentionally, they empower the men in their lives until those men have maximum influence over one of their most prized possessions—their self-esteem. This unplanned transfer of control very often becomes a key hindrance to a healthy and successful relationship.

It is not uncommon for black men to gain influence and power over a woman's self-esteem through compliments. Really! How you internalize your man's compliments can determine the course and quality of your relationship with him. On the one hand, if his compliments are a nice bonus and something you readily accept and like to hear, *but don't necessarily need*, you are in a position to have a healthy relationship. On the other hand, if you depend on your man's compliments to feel good about who you are, you could be setting yourself up for a very serious and negative situation. The end result is often a predictable collapse in your relationship, usually followed by an additional decrease in your self-confidence. Being aware of this disastrous sequence can help you avoid it.

Usually a man's compliments are not intended to have negative consequences, and he probably means what he says. In fact, what often happens is that most men will cater to your self-esteem, particularly in the early stages of a relationship, and especially before they have established a sexual union with you. This is a very normal and ordinary process. Quite naturally you feel good about the positive things a man says about you, and well you should.

Nevertheless, it is because of those positive comments and compliments that many black women are lured into relating what they feel about themselves to what he says and does. It's great when his words are uplifting, but in the process he gradually begins to have significant influence over their self-esteem. Even a man with good intentions can hold a woman's self-esteem hostage if she becomes dependent on him to feel good about herself.

A man may begin to have control over a woman's self-esteem because he is the first to consistently say good things about her. And she may get hooked on the compliments and attempt to avoid any negative statements from him. She may also not feel very good about herself and so desires to hear something positive from her man.

A problem will arise if the man who compliments you is still negatively influenced by the black male sexual image. On the one hand, that influence could be a hidden factor that surfaces from time to time and gets him to say something insensitive, degrading, or disrespectful. His words might do just enough damage to momentarily disrupt any positive perception you have of yourself. Over time this can have an accumulative effect on your self-esteem that becomes permanent. On the other hand, the negative black male sexual image can have such an extreme influence that he is likely to have very little or no respect for you or black women in general. From such a man you will get a constant barrage of negativism. Unless you challenge him, your entire relationship may become nothing more than a game to him.

In either case, in an unnoticed twist of fate, the man who may have given you confidence in the first place or who used to be full of praise and compliments now has you questioning your self-worth and perhaps feeling depressed—all because you gave him too much power to influence your self-worth with his compliments.

Furthermore, it only takes one bad experience of this type to leave some black women in doubt or with low self-esteem for many years, if not for life.

Cheri admits that she is constantly hoping that her man will not criticize her. "If he says anything negative about me," she explains, "it can have an influence on me for hours, days, even months. I want him to accept me for who I am. I feel rejected when he criticizes me." She doesn't realize that this attitude empowers him with control over her self-love. And with that kind of influence, he could make or break her.

You can see an example of low self-esteem in black women who otherwise have it together in every area of their life except the "man department." Indeed, if it were not for past relationships with certain black men, their perception of their total self-worth would be much higher.

In many cases, the problem can be so overwhelming that it bears negative consequences on other facets of their lives, such as how they raise their children, how effective they are on the job, or how they communicate to men in general. They often lose their ability to give a confident smile and say hello to a black man in passing.

Many such women go from relationship to relationship with little confidence and with each experience causing them to have less self-esteem. Oftentimes they will go to the next man and almost immediately give him the power to influence their self-esteem—hoping that he will validate them with his compliments. If he doesn't, or if he stops complimenting them at some point, they again start to have negative thoughts about themselves that adversely impact the relationship.

Of course, there are other factors that can cause a woman to have low self-esteem. She could be telling herself negative things that have nothing to do with black men. Or she may have thought that having sex would hold a relationship together, and when that fails she begins to feel less valuable. Several experiences with sexships will reinforce low self-esteem, as well as the fact that black men want sex but it is not what they are looking for.

Damage to a woman's self-esteem can be even more penetrating to one who bonds with entertainment interest rather than common interest because she is often under the illusion that entertainment interest is the only basis necessary for long-term quality commitment. But there probably is nothing more devastating to a black woman's self-esteem than when she loves her man more than he loves her, and he walks away. Suffering from any of these situations can make a black woman a prime candidate to be manipulated by a man's compliments. Among the duped, many let themselves go physically so that they can have a visible excuse. To them it might seem less painful if they give him what appears to be an obvious reason to tear down their self-esteem.

It's a catch-22 situation. If any of these women are to ever again have a consistent quality relationship, maintaining positive self-esteem is mandatory. They must come to realize that healthy self-esteem is not only a prized possession because of what it means to them personally, but it is usually a necessary factor for getting more love—or *any* love—from black men.

Fair or not, how much self-esteem you have influences how much love you get from black men. Certainly, a black man wants to perceive you as valuable, but ultimately that has to come from you.

It is very important to remember that what a black man does not tell a black woman is that the growth of his love invariably depends upon his perception that you love and value yourself. Conversely, your having low self-esteem will hinder the growth of his love, even if you feel that he is the one who caused you to feel negatively about yourself in the first place.

Actually, there is very little about the black male sexual image that connotes building or nurturing a woman's self-esteem or having empathy for a woman with low self-esteem. If anything, she is fair game and a prime candidate for a sexship, but not commitment to a long-term quality relationship. Indeed, if ever there was a golden rule regarding what most black men (even those heavily influenced by the negative black male sexual image) will succumb to, it is: "Love and respect are given to those women who love and respect themselves."

The truth is that black men are usually disappointed if they are interested in you and then come to realize that you have low self-esteem. Many will surely find a way to end the relationship.

What black men do when a woman has low self-esteem will often depend on two factors: (1) how much he is influenced by the negative black male sexual image, and (2) how much you will take before *you* end the relationship. It is often during this "how much you will take" phase that the greatest damage is done to your self-esteem.

Black men who stay in relationships with women who have low self-esteem often have their own self-esteem problems. Nevertheless, in such relationships these men are often more chauvinistic, less respectful, and more controlling of the woman. It is here that one can see the most obvious influence of the negative black male sexual image on a black man. When black men are communicating on this level, it is not uncommon for them to constantly find ways to tell a woman that she is undeserving and undesirable. The more she accepts his negative influence on her self-esteem, the less likely she is to seek change.

Furthermore, infidelity and lack of commitment are almost always a part of the relationship. He usually has other women, not only because he lacks respect for her, but also because he knows she doesn't feel worthy enough or capable of doing anything about it. This too can be a very sensitive and volatile situation for a woman, because once some black men are committed to this lifestyle, they can be very controlling and refuse to let go of the relationship. When that is the case, the woman is well advised to seek professional help.

Nevertheless, to avoid the problems mentioned in this chapter, a black woman must first be keenly aware that the quality of her relationship with *herself* is directly related to the quality of her relationship with her man. Secondly, a black woman who has allowed a black man to determine what she feels about herself must wake up! If he can build you up, he can tear you down! Accept the buildup—it's probably true. But reject the teardown even if it is. Certainly, a man can be right in both his compliments and his criticisms, but neither should determine your self-value. If he has what you feel is a legitimate complaint about you, that's fine. You either need to make the change or accept it. But allowing him to control your self-esteem can truly turn you into your own worst enemy.

Black men are looking for and committing to women with a confident sense of self! Let that be *you*, and his love will increase. You must know you are valuable simply because you are you. Period! If you can't accept this fact and you are not in a relationship, you should avoid getting into one until you can accept it.

Undoubtedly, you must wisely avoid letting your man's compliments govern your self-worth, particularly with a man who is or can suddenly be influenced by the negative black male sexual image. Never again be that insecure or foolish!

CHAPTER 8

❄

Rediscovering a Valuable Asset

Attracting your man or any black man can be an effortless endeavor when using the right amount of the right ingredients. One such ingredient is counted among the many things God has given women. It is one very special and valuable asset that—without fail—powerfully attracts a man.

Stay with me on this one, because when this asset is used properly, most black men will surrender themselves to you unconditionally. As if you were a magnet, they will keep coming back just to be around you and to experience the power of it. And while every black woman has it, they don't all know how to use it. In fact, many need to adjust what they have in order to take maximum advantage of it.

That very powerful and captivating asset is none other than your femininity. Don't dare underestimate what to some men, at its most potent level, is the eighth wonder of the world.

Femininity does to a man's eyes what a delicious fragrance does to his nose. In fact, femininity is so much like a fragrance to a man that it has the same effect. Too little of it, and he will not notice you. Too much of it, and he will turn away. But use the right amount, and he'll keep wanting to come back to your femininity as if hypnotized by a captivating fragrance.

Now could be the time to rediscover your femininity and harness its power. The woman who does this is virtually guaranteed to have success with attracting her man again or for the first time. If you have tried to use femininity on a man and felt it did not work, it might be because you didn't use the right amount. In this section you will learn what the right amount is. You might think that it works on only a select few black men. But, to the contrary, most black men will subject themselves to the power of your femininity—when it is used properly.

Femininity can be defined as the quality or nature of the female sex. Black men are naturally attracted to femininity because it is the opposite of what they are supposed to be. One of nature's most basic laws is that opposites attract. Black men are attracted to your femininity because you have exclusive rights to it. It is yours, and they can't have it. Yet they want it and they look for it in a woman. Besides, the one acceptable way they can relate to the black male sexual image and get in touch with their own delicate nature is through you.

If you don't already, you must come to know and understand the value of your femininity. When you do, you will *have* to feel good about who you are. Femininity is best brought out when you love and feel good about yourself. A woman who loves herself has high self-esteem and thus values her sex, sexuality, and femininity. I guarantee you that the woman who feels good about herself carries herself in a way that displays femininity, and that demeanor attracts men.

Since femininity is the quality or nature of the female sex, it is best represented by things that are usually off-limits to men. For instance, high heels, ankle bracelets, leg warmers, nylon stockings, polished nails, lingerie, hair styles, softness, certain body language, movements, and styles of clothing are all things closely associated with women. Thus, when you display them in a feminine fashion, they attract men.

Breasts represent femininity because they, too, are something that men don't have. If you have small breasts, you can play up your other feminine qualities and men will be attracted to you. On the other hand, if you have small breasts and because of them you play down your other feminine qualities, you may have a difficult time attracting men. You may be thinking it's because of your breasts, when in fact it's because you play down your femininity.

The same can be said about skin color. If your skin is very dark or very light, and you are negatively affected in a way so that you can't be confidently feminine, you will attract less men. You will be thinking that you attract fewer men because of your skin color, when in reality that's not the reason at all.

Since black men look for femininity, they are more likely to commit to a woman with the right mix of femininity and not necessarily the one who has the best looks. Although it can be said that if a woman *thinks* she looks good, she is also likely to be displaying femininity.

For many black women, their femininity has been seriously undermined by their basic need to survive. For some, that has meant taking on masculine qualities to survive in the workplace. Others maintain that they have had to be tough, hard, or cold just to relate to black men. They don't realize that if a man aims to lower their self-esteem, he has less of a target when they feel good about their femininity. Then there are those women who believe that being a contemporary woman has nothing to with feminine qualities. They downplay, denigrate, or simply ignore their feminine attributes.

But you should enjoy and celebrate your femininity because it's the essence of who you are. There is no doubt that black men are less attracted to women who have lost their sense of femininity. You know that this is the case any time you look like, dress like, act like, or smell like a man, regardless of how you justify it. Furthermore, being a mother does not excuse a woman from being feminine any more than being a father excuses a man from being masculine. A black woman who wears practically anything almost anywhere does not take advantage of the power of her femininity. On the other hand, a woman who wears an ankle bracelet or who adds leg warmers to a sweat suit might be using the influence of femininity to its maximum potential.

Certainly, loud and aggressive behavior is primarily associated with masculinity. Therefore, when a woman displays it, that is exactly how men will perceive it—as masculine behavior. The other extreme is not much better; that is, when a woman uses femininity as an excuse to be weak or fragile, mentally or otherwise. Although men feel that femininity can be doll-like, it does not mean being a perfect little doll. Too much femininity can also turn a man off.

There are many black women who have had to do tough jobs but were able to still maintain feminine qualities. Jackie Joyner-Kersee displayed powerful public femininity as she broke world track records, and men were obviously attracted to her. Carol Moseley Braun became the first black congresswoman from Illinois in the same manner.

Do you have oomph? It is defined as personal charm, magnetism, glamour, sex appeal, and vitality. Certainly, it is a good thing to display feminine qualities, but when you display them with style, you have oomph. Being a woman with oomph suggests that you like being a woman. No doubt femininity has even greater power when it is displayed by women with oomph.

If femininity were a fine-tuned race car, oomph would be the gas that makes a difference in its power. Women who have oomph usually achieve consistent femininity through their personality, attitude, style of dress, and even their hair style. When those things are all brought together, they have what defines oomph: personal charm, magnetism, glamour, sex appeal, and vitality.

Because oomph is consistent femininity, it guarantees that you will attract black men. In fact, attracting your man a second time or attracting a man for the first time can be easy for women who display the majestic disposition called oomph.

Moreover, like femininity, you can test the power of oomph and see its influence on the man in your life. Then you will plainly see that black men are attracted to women who have and communicate it—even if you and your man have been together for years, and he knows you very well and knows what you look like at your best as well as at your worst. The power of femininity is always available to you. Don't forget that while relationships can appear to be unchanged, they are constantly in transition.

There are times when you accidentally or naturally use the power of femininity on your man. That's when you put on certain clothes, or wear your hair in a particular style, or act a certain way. The results are usually the same—he wants you!

There is nothing wrong with being deliberate about the way you display your femininity. Determine what feminine qualities you would like to accent and use them to attract your man. Show some oomph by doing it consistently. Let him connect to his feminine side through you.

You can always measure to see if you are using the right amount of femininity on the man in your life. Its power will be evident in his behavior. When you have the right amount, he will stare at you, touch you, and want to be around you. You need to increase your femininity when he's not doing those things. Conversely, you need to reduce your femininity when he wants you at those times that you want space. Make no mistake about it, the use of femininity will move you higher on his Love Scale.

CHAPTER 9

✳

The Claire Huxtable Attitude

Sensuously she stands at the top of the stairs. Her eyes warmly pierce through his nonchalant attitude. The look on her face would later be duplicated by the rising sun. The slender soft finger next to her thumb is tantalizingly and intimately inviting him, her husband, to retire early.

His eyes rekindled and began to sparkle like evaporating morning dew. Rhythmically his eyebrows rolled as if they were warm Hawaiian waves gently kissing the shore. A daunting smile shimmered across his face like the flicker of fluorescent lights. His facial expression began to mimic that of a child on Christmas morning. Then suddenly he became sophisticated and suave, and his head began to sway desirously. He knew what time it was! And that's how I see the ending of any one episode of the *Cosby Show*.

It was one of the most popular black TV series ever. Almost everyone who watched it enjoyed and quite often learned something from it. But there was more to be learned than those lessons that might have been immediately obvious. One lesson in particular could tell you what's wrong with the sex in your marriage and could save or revive a dying sexual relationship.

Although black men are not looking for sex, their sexual desire for you can influence the quality of your marriage. One of the worst things any woman can do in a marriage is to use sex to manipulate her man. Although many do it, such actions can create more problems than they solve. Manipulation often leads to a relationship in which you are plainly saying with your sexuality, "If you don't live up to my expectations, whatever they may be, I will not have sex with you."

If the truth is to be known, that kind of attitude and behavior is not consistently tolerated when considering the black male image and the many black men who define themselves by it. The one thing that black men are supposed to control, if not outright master, is *your* sexuality. Many black men believe that your body belongs to them by way of your relationship. Thus, they feel there shouldn't be any manipulation and very little control on your part because that would imply that you are the owner of your sexuality. If you try to show ownership by saying no to his sexual advances and you have no real physical reason, some black men will attempt to show you that they will not be denied. They are usually unaware that they are attempting to live up to the chauvinistic aspect of the black male image. Such a situation could escalate into many serious problems.

But if we return our attention back to the *Cosby Show*,

we can examine the Claire Huxtable Attitude. If you will recall, almost any time that there was the implication that Mr. and Mrs. Huxtable were about to get sexually involved, he would act very excited. His reaction would go from childlike to debonair in a matter of seconds, and we would all laugh.

If we take another look at the *Cosby Show*, we might see a few things about Claire Huxtable's attitude that are rather valuable. Interestingly enough, what's implied about her attitude is a primary part of what will keep a black man desiring you, and desiring you, and desiring you, throughout your relationship.

Oftentimes when a woman is in a committed relationship and gets married, she feels that her man belongs to her and that she belongs to him. Our point of focus is the "she belongs to him" attitude, because usually that attitude includes the "it belongs to him" attitude, with *it* being her sex. Probably out of a sense of duty as well as the goodness of her heart and a desire to please her man, her message to him is: Here is my body; it belongs to you.

At first thought, that message of her sex belongs to him may seem appropriate because, after all, she is his. In theory, there should be nothing wrong with the idea. But in reality there is a problem, and it has a very good chance of becoming a major dilemma that will influence the quality of your relationship. The "it belongs to him" attitude can be enough to turn your man completely off and cause him to have less desire for you sexually.

When a woman takes the "it belongs to him" attitude, that is exactly what a man, particularly a husband, will expect. In fact, many black men will say things that express their ownership, such as "Where have you been with my stuff?" Or "I want some of my stuff tonight." Or the favorite, "You better not give my stuff away." In many cases, it does not matter what kind of attitude you have, or who controls it; some black men will still make statements that express their ownership.

Furthermore, when you have the "it belongs to him" attitude, most men will start to lose significant desire for "it" over a period of time. A primary reason is because that attitude means he has far too much psychological access, and he feels he can have "it" at will and almost anytime he wants. If he thinks he has total access, what generally happens is that each time his sexual desire starts to build (even if just a little), at an opportune moment he's going to want to satisfy himself. Rarely will he take the time to let his desire for you build.

One reason he is going to want sex whenever he has the desire is because there is little or nothing about the black male sexual image that suggests sexual moderation. Indeed, the opposite message is associated with the image that says, "Be foot loose and fancy free and get it whenever you have a chance." Remember, the message black men get is, "You are a black male; express your sexuality." Consequently, most black men don't learn to discipline themselves when it comes to sexual desire.

Thus, when they have any desire, they want to act on it.

If your man can have sex with you anytime he wants, eventually he will probably burn himself out physically or mentally—causing him to have a loss of sexual desire for you. The physical burnout is often ephemeral. The mental burnout is where the real problem lies. Outside of marriage, a typical black man's attitude is "Chase it until you get it." The moment he succeeds, he may psychologically stop wanting it as much, or wanting it at all. The psychological equivalent of this in marriage is when "it" totally belongs to him. At first, he is happy and proud to have "it." But once it becomes his to control, the chances are that he will eventually lose interest.

A typical warning sign is when he shows you, on a consistent basis, that he's only interested in sexually satisfying himself. If you recall, that's not how he started out. He used to be concerned about your satisfaction. Now he's at a point where he only satisfies himself. Remember, "it" belongs to him. In most cases, he will begin to feel that since "it" is his, he really doesn't have to satisfy you to get "it." When that happens, sooner or later you are not going to want to give "it" to him, because you're being neglected.

This may even put you in the manipulative mode— which is to say, "Satisfy me or I will resist having sex with you." If he tries to satisfy you, it may be a temporary fix because, remember again, "it" is his. If you have given sex to him anytime and almost anywhere he wanted it, he has become accustomed to getting "it" that way, and will likely fall back into his old pattern.

Moreover, if your desire exceeds his, you are in a prime position for him to eventually lose interest in you altogether. Why? Because this, too, usually means he has total access to you. Psychologically, he thinks he controls "it." He knows that you're always ready when he's ready, and he will be satisfied to the limits of his desire. In many ways, it's like anything else. For example, if you love chocolate ice cream and you're able to have some every time you have the slightest desire, you will eventually lose interest. On the other hand, if you thought you couldn't have it every time you wanted some (even if you could), whenever you do have chocolate ice cream you are more likely to enjoy the moment.

I reiterate that it's psychological access and who your man believes controls "it" that has impact—not whether or not you say yes to his advances or how often you have sex together.

Who desires whom more is almost always psychological and is based on how you psychologically position yourself in the relationship. If you desire him more, it is because at some point in your relationship you made that decision and started to live the part.

Men have been socialized to give value to a woman's sex. Ironically, some men give more value to it than the woman does. Even so, the psychological work has been done for you. If your man does not value your sex, it's usually because you have not seemed to value it yourself. By the way, that's the only prerequisite—if it seems valuable to you, it will automatically be valuable to him.

As you will discover, with the Claire Huxtable Attitude, he believes consciously or unconsciously that you are in psychological control of your body. Subsequently, it adds value to "it" and to his experience. Hence, his desire for you increases. The result is a man who does not quite feel that he can totally satisfy his desire for you, no matter how often he gets "it." The whole idea amounts to increased love and enjoyment for all involved.

There are plenty of women who have greater sexual desire for their men than the men have for them but who have the men believing that *they* have the greater desire. Many of these women start by making their man feel that he has little or no control over her "it." Consequently, he can't leave her alone.

To further make the point, some women experience an increase in attentiveness and increased sexual desire on the part of their male partner during a breakup. It's during that time that they take back control over "it," and he psychologically wants to regain it. There are women who tell stories of men who try to control and/or own "it" years after a breakup. It is important to note that if the only time you take control over "it" is during disputes, that's manipulation. Keep in mind that I am talking about an attitude. Once you have assured a black man that he controls "it," and not you, and that he can do with it pretty much as he pleases, it can be rather difficult for him to stop believing otherwise. But if you choose to, getting him to see that you are in control of your body can certainly be done. It can be done with a change in your attitude and ultimately with a change in your actions. If you try to tell him, rather than show him with your actions, he probably won't believe what you say.

Furthermore, if you try to tell black men that you are now in control of "it," not only will it sound ridiculous to them, but many will outright and openly resist. Some will accuse you of trying to break up the relationship, seeing someone else, losing interest, being too aggressive and taking over the man's role, or forcing them to look to other women, and so on.

Ironically, while black men desire you to have control over your body, they are constantly trying to take control so that they can have "it" anytime they have an urge. And once they have control, they are usually opposed to giving it back. The problem again is that they remain in control until they lose interest. But if you have the right attitude, you can take control and have them loving you more because you did so. More than anything, the way you assert ownership can determine your effectiveness and make the difference.

Now here comes Claire Huxtable teaching America's women the way to do it and the right attitude to have. Right there on what was America's number one family show. Plus, I will take the liberty to go behind the scenes to paint a more lucid picture.

Claire's attitude suggested, "My stuff is mine, sweetheart. But because you are my husband, guess what? You can have some." And Cliff Huxtable would get as happy as he could be. His wife was *giving* him some! You could tell that he wasn't controlling her "stuff," or he would not have acted so happy. If he had been in control, he probably would have burned that kind of happiness out long ago. Maybe she also understands that men in general like to engage in sex that belongs to someone else. When your man is with you, and you have the Claire Huxtable Attitude, it has the effect of him engaging in sex that belongs to someone else. This is a psychological difference about which you would be wise to take special note.

The Claire Huxtable Attitude is just that—an attitude that manifests itself in her actions. She didn't argue with her man about who owned or controlled "it." Nor did she make him feel that he was not desired when she turned him down. She had a very loving attitude, in contrast to a mean, negative, or nasty one—which, of course, can be a turnoff.

There was no doubt that her "stuff" would be given only to him—when she was ready to do so. Her attitude was, "I love you, but I also love *me*, and I feel good enough about myself to not let you take 'it' over." Thus, she controlled "it" out of respect for herself.

Women who use their sex to manipulate their man send the message, "As long as you act right or I can have my way, you can have my sex whenever you want it." Men have far less respect for this because they realize that they are being manipulated. Plus, those men who have bad intentions often act right just long enough to get what they want and/or to burn themselves out.

With the Claire Huxtable Attitude, things don't have to be going wrong for you to be in control. She is constantly giving and seeking respect—not manipulating. Her attitude says: "I am confident, responsible, caring, loving, and understanding. Sometimes I have problems that I will need you to handle, but regardless, my sexuality is mine. I control it. And because I love you, and you are my husband, I will give you permission to have it either by my actions or my words, or both, almost anywhere, almost anytime! But I don't want you to ever feel that you can have it whenever and do with it whatever you want."

She does not take the attitude: "We have done it before. What's the big deal? It's all the same anyway, since sex is sex." That attitude causes you to relinquish psychological value.

With Claire's attitude, when Mr. Huxtable gets home from work and he's desirous, he usually gets "it," but he does not always know if she's going to give "it" to him. He's clear about who controls "his stuff." He remembers there were a few times when he was in the mood and she had some work to do or she simply wasn't in the mood. She didn't make up headache or cramp stories. She just told him very lovingly and nicely that then was not the time. Oh, he would act up sometimes if she said no, because his desire would influence him that way. But ultimately he respected her enough to wait, and he understood that "it" was hers, even though he still called "it" his.

Certainly, there were times when Mrs. Huxtable would change her mind because he playfully encouraged her mood. But she let him have "it" because he got her in the mood. Men will take more time to get you in the mood if they think you might say no and that they have to respect your wish.

There may have been times when Claire attracted him by wearing something sexy and paying him little attention as she went about her business. She confidently knew that eventually he would summit to her femininity, and with increased desire.

Another example of how one woman added psychological value to her sexuality can be seen in Tamara's routine. She had an attitude like Claire's. From time to time, her man would want sex, and she would let him know in a loving way that she was pampering her body and her sex. She would turn on soft music, and relax in a bubble bath, and do her nails. The thought of her caring for "his stuff," coupled with the fact that he had to wait, would drive him nearly crazy with desire. He would want to get in the tub with her. He would complain about her taking too long. Sometimes he would change his mind because she made him wait. But none of that bothered Tamara, because she knew he would return with added passion.

The unending result is that the Mr. Huxtables of the world will complain simply to test your ability to maintain control. But when they see that you are lovingly persistent, they will continue to romance and satisfy you. No matter how much access your man has had in the past, when you're in control, he will consistently romance and satisfy you because he will want you to say yes to his sexual advances.

The Claire Huxtable Attitude will not only make him desire and love you more, but you will shine like the royalty you are.

CHAPTER 10

❄

The Green-Eyed Monster

Dripping with power and cracking with energy, the super charge of jealousy could find its way into your relationship and give it an exceptionally gratifying boost. No need to pull down the curtains or come any closer, I'll whisper loudly. You should have a clear understanding of the effects that jealousy can have on a black man and an even clearer understanding of how to use its piercing power.

Based primarily on who controls it and ultimately how it is used, the power of jealousy, like nuclear power, can be exceptionally menacing. Similarly, if misappropriated, the consequences can be disastrous.

You might initially think that harnessing the power of jealousy and using it to your benefit is unfair play. But in this context there are no immoral intentions. Thus, whether or not you should consider using the power of jealousy should depend not on your morals but on your situation. If your situation is right for its use, you might find it quite a handy fixer-upper.

For many people who feel jealousy, the issue of morality is only a cover for their hurt feelings. It's an experience that is sometimes described as a strange and funny feeling. People have a problem with jealousy because they know it can feel like going off the deep end of a roller coaster and staying there longer than you care to. Your heart climbs to your neck, the racing of blood causes a sudden surge in body temperature, and your thoughts bounce back and forth like a racquet ball. You might try to avoid that strange funny feeling by telling yourself that the best thing for you to do is to be calm and quiet as you breathe a little deeper, trying to make up for what sometimes seems like a loss of vital oxygen. Deep down you know that jealousy is forcing your inner body to do the funky chicken, and you simply don't like it.

Another reason people are opposed to deliberately using jealousy to enhance their relationship is that it is all too often associated with negative and tactless use. For example, a woman at a social gathering might give a man an inviting glance, and when he responds she then super-ficially engages him in dialogue. His initial hopes are dashed when he realizes that she enticed him over only to make her man jealous as he returns from the bathroom. The more obvious it is that jealousy is contrived, the less appealing it is. In this situation, even if the woman's trick makes her man jealous, the jealousy is usually ephemeral at best, in part because she doesn't know how to take full advantage of it.

Okay, so is it wrong to deliberately make your man feel jealous, or not? Yes, it can be wrong to deliberately make him feel jealous when he loves and respects you and demonstrates it properly. But even then, if he happens to get jealous over, say, another man showing interest in you, then you might as well react in a fashion that will use the power of jealousy to your benefit. However, it is appropriate to focus on using jealousy when your relationship is in trouble and/or your man is taking you for granted. It might be that he is consistently out of line because your love for him is greater than his love for you.

While using jealousy can have an effect on some men, no matter where they are on the scale, the more love your man has for you, the more effective the use of jealousy is likely to be.

Nevertheless, if you rate your love for him at 7, and his love for you at 5, jealousy has the power to wake him or shake him up and immediately boost him to 8, 9, or 10. He might come down some after the initial boost, but, depending on the impact and how you handle it, he can continue loving you at a higher level for an extended period of time. Even a man who does not seem to care anymore can be brought to attention and forced to care more if you use the power of jealousy.

For optimum effect, jealousy should not be used as an isolated problem-solver in your relationship, but rather as one tool along with the others that you read about in this book. Only then can it become a viable and effective alternative with which to initiate the process of recovery from a sour or faltering relationship.

For instance, you can control the transition that takes place after a surge of jealousy that boosts your man up the Love Scale while you simultaneously go down the scale. You could also use the time to strengthen your relationship by establishing more common interests. Furthermore, if he attempts to play games, which is very likely during this transition, you should be on top of his every move in a very loving yet firm manner.

The effect that jealousy can have on black men is predictable because no one likes the idea of losing his woman to another man. It's a thought that stands squarely against everything the black male sexual image stands for. Your man's natural and instinctive response is to do what it takes to avoid this feeling and the loss.

Quite often a man's reaction to jealousy is to find a way to get you to feel more fear than he does, so that he can feel less. So he might rant and rave. But seldom does a man leave a relationship or end it because he has had the funny and strange feeling that jealousy can create. He might threaten to leave or threaten to get another woman, but as long as he's experiencing genuine jealousy, he's in a weak position, and the power of his jealousy won't let him leave. The exception is if you are constantly using jealousy as a tool to influence him. Then using jealousy might create too much of a roller-coaster relationship and provoke lasting negative feelings. In that case, your man is likely to leave because he feels insecure and believes that you will eventually be unfaithful regardless of what he does.

Still, it's natural and it's okay for a man to feel some fear during jealousy. It is often the emotion that some men *need* to feel.

Your reaction to a jealous man is critical. It will determine the impact of jealousy and set the tone for everything that follows. His grumbling only has power if you allow yourself to be negatively affected. Don't let his reaction cause you to panic or overreact.

The mistake some women make is that they attempt to ensure that their man never feel jealous. They go out of their way to persuade him that there is no cause for jealousy, when most of the time the man knows that but just wants reassurance. When he gets it, he is relieved because he doesn't have to suffer the anxiety of jealousy.

When Rodney asked Kelly about the friendliness demonstrated toward her by the handsome manager on her job, she knew he was feeling jealous. She calmly assured Rodney that she was interested only in him. But she didn't eradicate all Rodney's fear. The fear that remained kept Rodney asking questions and being on his toes.

Quite often the most effective way to respond to a jealous man is to calmly, lovingly, and respectfully give him the reassurance he needs in one short statement and leave it at that. What you are giving him is genuine reassurance, without dragging it out. If there is a need to repeat yourself so he can hear you, that's fine. Give the same statement in the same way, calmly, lovingly, and respectfully.

Claude, a brother who used to be known as a ladies' man, was shaken by jealousy one day when he was at a social gathering with his wife. Like many men rocked by the feeling of jealousy, he first became angry and then felt a need to get closer and more affectionate with his woman. After the incident, he held her hand, although he was generally opposed to doing so in public. And like many men who are jolted by jealousy, he had a hundred questions when they got home. He wouldn't say it, but he wanted reassurance that she was not going anywhere. Also, like many black men who are touched by jealousy, he felt an increased sexual desire. Plus, he thought that making love with his wife would give him a chance to exercise his sexual power to ensure that she wasn't going anywhere.

The impact of jealousy on a man is likely to be influenced most by two factors: (1) how the other man looks, and (2) what the other man's financial status appears to be. In other words, your man will feel the greatest impact from jealousy if he thinks that a better-looking man, who appears to have more income or status than he, is after you. Just one of those two factors can be effective, but when both factors apply, the impact is greater and usually very powerful.

The idea of using jealousy is based on a man desiring you, and not on you pursuing another man. The latter tends to create a negative feeling and reaction. Additionally, if you simply tell your man about someone he could be jealous of, but he's never seen that man, he might feel some jealousy; but seeing is believing and probably more effective.

One time when I was telling a woman about the power of jealousy, she asked if she would have the same impact on her noncommittal friend if she staged the "Mr. Handsome with money and/or status in hot pursuit" scenario. I said that she might be surprised at the results if she could have another man act out the scene properly. But to do it right meant that first she had to be absolutely sure that any other man brought onto the scene would not be brought into a hostile situation. Secondly, she had to create a scenario that would be first and foremost convincing beyond a doubt. To do it unconvincingly can make things worse because your man is likely to look for ways to pay you back.

There are a few negative aspects to using jealousy. With some men you have to be able to take what you give out. However, if you use the power of jealousy properly, you will not likely have to worry about him responding in a retaliatory manner. You also have to be cautious of men who become overly jealous. Not only can they get on your nerves, but jealousy can become their excuse to exhibit unpredictable and irrational reactionary behavior.

There are several occasions when you should avoid using jealousy altogether—for example, if you think, even for only a second, that the man you are using it on may have a violent tendency; or if he has ever gotten violent with you before, concerning this or other issues; or if you don't know enough about him to determine if he has a violent tendency. In any event, jealousy has the power to cause innate violent behavior to surface. Certainly, if you are trying to get rid of a man, avoid making him jealous, because he will want to stay with you even more.

Nevertheless, confident and sure that her man was nonviolent and that she knew someone who could help her carry the whole thing off properly, Sherry set out to shake her relationship with a jolt of jealousy. She was in a relationship with a man who always seemed to be on the verge of making a commitment but didn't seem to be able to bring himself to it. She needed to boost him a little higher on the Love Scale. So instead of making herself appear more attractive in the traditional way, with makeup, she decided to use another man and the impact of jealousy. She used a simple one-time scenario. Sherry had her noncommittal friend over at her place, and they were preparing dinner when the doorbell rang as planned. When she opened the door, there stood a handsome, well-dressed man in casual clothes with one flower in his hand. He apologized for coming unannounced. She asked him in, introduced him to her friend, and then she and Mr. Handsome went outside and talked for about five minutes. When she came back inside, her friend responded as many black men would.

Mr. Noncommittal played it cool, and so did she. She came in inquiring about dinner and offered no explanation. Sure enough, during dinner he started his question session by casually asking where they had met. In the days that followed, after any time she had been missing, he often made comments suggesting that she was out with Mr. Handsome. Thus, the jealousy continued to affect him for some time. It was not long before she got the commitment she wanted and continues to have.

For good measure, she had Mr. Handsome call her once on the phone while her man was there, and she respectfully told Mr. Handsome no to his request for a date. It was important that she treated her suitor with respect so that her man would think that he had a chance with her.

In another situation involving jealousy, Rhonda had Roger pursue her on an ongoing basis. This kept Brian on his toes, which she believed was an influencing factor in his later willingness to commit.

Obviously, there are many more incidents in which jealousy has made men do the right thing. So don't be afraid to be unconventional. Use the power of the green-eyed-monster.

CHAPTER 11

❄

The Boogey Man Theory

You look under the bed and in the closet. Then you tell your child to stop crying—that there is no boogey man in his room, and there's no such thing as a boogey man anyway. But as soon as you turn out the lights and close the door, he starts to cry again, and understandably so. The child is probably thinking, if there's no boogey man, what were you looking for? Why did you look under my bed and in my closet? The mere fact that you looked probably suggested to him that the boogey man hides when you are looking and will come to get him when he's alone in the dark.

The boogey man theory minus the boogey becomes "the other man" theory. The two are comparable in that "the other man" theory can have the same effect on a man that the boogey man theory can have on a child. If a man accuses you of playing or messing around when that simply is not the case, the issue is often best settled without you dignifying his charge by attempting to prove your innocence.

When you are innocent, very often the more you try to

convince him that you are, the more he thinks you aren't. Some black men have been known to accuse women of "incidents," knowing for the most part that they are innocent, or at least hoping they are. The accusation is their way of checking up on you. Whether or not your man will continue with his charge or intensify his belief depends, for the most part, on your reaction. What he really wants is reassurance that you still love and desire only him. But like the child who is convinced that there is a boogey man because he sees you looking for one, your man may wonder why you go through so much to prove your innocence if his accusations have no basis.

Now, this kind of game-playing may upset you, and you may even ask why he would play such a childish game. It's a crude system, but men are not as advanced on checking up as most women are. Actually, it's the result and not the process that matters to him. By approaching you in this fashion, he can gain what might be valid information about any possible tendencies toward infidelity. The problem is that you may not know what he's up to, and the method may cause more problems than it solves.

Charles went to his wife Carla's office party. He saw Noel, a handsome young man who worked with Carla, appear to whisper something to her. Knowing nothing else about their relationship and fearing that something might be going on between them, he politely accused her of having a crush on Noel. A few minutes later, he upgraded that concern to a possible affair. Carla tried to explain to Charles that his words were simply not true. In doing so, she explained that she and Noel were in different departments, worked different shifts, and rarely saw each other. But by night's end, she and Charles were barely speaking as a result of his charges.

Carla had indeed been telling the truth. She barely knew Noel, and, more important to Charles, she had no interest in him. She knew that Charles was being ridiculous. However, she would have handled the situation much better if she hadn't worked so hard to prove that there was no (boogey man) relationship between her and Noel. The key is that the accusation was so ridiculous that it didn't deserve all the attention she gave it. Focusing on it helped to increase the fantasy in Charles's mind.

What Carla should have done was be concise yet respectful and serious. She might have ended the whole fiasco by saying, "Noel and I are co-workers. You are my husband." Even with that said, Charles might have raised the issue again, but probably not with as much fervor. In any event, Carla's best course of action would have been not to defend the ridiculous.

On the other hand, if Carla did have a secret relationship with Noel, this approach probably wouldn't work, for several reasons. First of all, Charles is likely to sense more and feel much stronger about the accusation. And second, unless Carla is a superb actress, she probably won't seem nearly as sincere when she attempts to make what is real sound ridiculous. To most men, if you act or appear guilty, you *are* until he takes you through enough changes to make himself feel better.

At any rate, if there is a genuine cause for concern, your man, like a frightened child, is not likely to drop the issue easily. But when the truth is on your side, it's usually better to avoid long explanations when trying to say there's no "bogey man" or "other man." In both instances, your relationship is likely to be better.

In fact, if you have nothing to hide, and if you respond appropriately, he will never admit it, and his initial actions will probably not reveal it, but he is likely to fall slightly deeper in love with you, out of genuine jealousy.

CHAPTER 12

❄

He Should Know

At the risk of appearing to overemphasize the obvious, I feel it is absolutely necessary to say that black men *cannot* read your mind. It does not matter how perfect and magnificent he appears. It does not matter how wonderful and glorious you are. It does not matter how in-sync the two of you are. The conclusion is the same: black men cannot read your mind!

I stress this point not because black women are consistently expecting black men to read their minds, but because too many times I have known black women who do not speak up on issues of concern to them. Seemingly, they can tell everybody but the man who needs to hear the problem. They often stubbornly and insistently claim, "I shouldn't have to say anything." Or, "He should have known how I was feeling." Or, "He doesn't know what to do. Why should I have to teach him?" Or, "I wish I had a more sensitive man."

Obviously, he should know the difference between what's right and wrong or what's respectful and disrespectful. But do not rely on him to know what you are thinking and how you feel about issues that matter to you.

In many ways, when you expect him to know what you're thinking or what to do to satisfy you, you are stereotyping him. Perhaps you are wanting him to perform up to the black male sexual image that you have heard about. But naturally you only want the positive side. Anything less is a disappointment to you. Maybe you want him to perform up to the image of the romantically sensitive black man, and he falls short of your expectations. If that's the case, you must put aside your expectations and communicate your desires.

Quite often when black women have a man that they feel is not sensitive enough, they don't want to teach or tell him how he should be. They expect him to know. However, blocking emotions is more in line with the black male image than tuning into them. Men in general, of all races, grow up learning to block out their emotions. Thus, at the times you are expecting sensitivity from your man, it is possible that he's blocking out his own emotions, not to mention yours. Furthermore, telling some black men what you want (several times) is not enough. Your goal should be to communicate until your man consistently demonstrates with his actions that he understands your message.

Some of the problem may be due in part to the fact that some black women are very intuitive and quite good at tuning into what's on a man's mind. Therefore, they expect the same of him. But don't rely on "he should know" or mind reading as a source of communication. If you do, you'll be setting yourself up for miscommunication, which leads to bad communication, which can ultimately lead to numerous other problems—problems that can be avoided. You may think that if you are not feeling well, he should be able to tune in to that, particularly after you have told him you aren't well. Maybe he should know that now is your time for soup in bed; but instead, he's focused on a ball game. Maybe he should know that he hurt your feelings with that stupid joke; but instead, he continues to tease you.

What sometimes can happen when a black man doesn't tune in or isn't sensitive to an issue is that many black women become angry, go into a silent mode, give him the cold shoulder, or become overly nice when they are actually boiling inside.

Whether your issue is large or small, if you are feeling sensitive about it, your sensitivity may be why you are hesitating to say what you feel. Yet, it is during this very time that communication is most important. To make matters worse, there will be times when you *do* say what you feel, and he still doesn't relate to the level of emotions associated with your words.

Don't be discouraged. Or perhaps more important, don't let discouragement lower you into expecting him to know what you feel and think, when what you really want or should be doing is communicating. Expecting a man to know what's on your mind is not communication at all.

The evidence for this is the number of women who complain that this expectation gets them nowhere. The thing to remember is that when communication fails, the solution lies in finding methods for improving it.

You would be equally mistaken in trying to read his mind. Some black men have the women in their lives conditioned so that the women don't or won't discuss certain issues. Instead, they try to read their man's mind. To do so suggests to him that you are weak, and it opens the door for him to play many games.

Do not let your relationship disintegrate to the point that you allow yourself to communicate to your man by attempting to guess what's on his mind. Rather, use "being in tune" as a way to determine what issues to talk about. For example, if you feel that his recent change in behavior indicates a lack of respect for you or that he might be seeing another woman, don't wimp out. Instead, calmly and firmly, in a respectful, no-nonsense kind of way, address the issue as soon as you can.

Surely, you cannot expect to live a happy, rewarding life with a man who can get away with excuses as to why he cannot communicate with you properly. The truth is, men *do* talk to women—women with whom they are at least on the same level on the Love Scale.

CHAPTER 13

❄

Moody Waters

Moody and overly sensitive people usually get their way. That's often why they're moody and overly sensitive in the first place. They have learned that their moods can manipulate others to more readily do what they desire. But such behavior can have significant effects on a relationship. It often starts in childhood and is carried over into adulthood.

Many people will announce at some point in their relationship with you that they are moody or very sensitive. The underlying reason is to prepare you to respond in accordance with their moods and sensitivity. They are at their best when you fully understand their message and begin to let them have their way and/or manipulate you because of their condition.

People who use moodiness and sensitivity as a means of communication (or to avoid communication) usually detract from the quality of their overall relationships. While things may seem to work out for them, in that they can influence the behavior of people around them, their approach is very selfish. That's why most people would rather not be around a moody or overly sensitive person. When you have to live with a person who maintains such behavior, it stifles the communication process, and this can suffocate your relationship. This behavior allows the person to avoid dealing with certain problems by simply claiming that the problems affect either their mood or sensitivity.

Emotions come and go, but you have *them*, they don't have *you*. That means that you can also put emotions down. When you handle your emotions maturely, you are able to put them aside and think clearly. Of course, there are people who really do need professional psychological help in this area, and they should seek it. Others have learned to mimic real psychological problems, and many of these people start to actually believe in their own act. If they are true to themselves, very often it's a matter of realizing that they aren't as moody or as sensitive as they profess to be. If nothing else, they have the ability to pay attention to their mood swings and direct their reactions. To do so helps to take the destructive aspect of sensitivity and mood manipulation out of a relationship. Furthermore, it improves communication on tough issues—not just for the moody and overly sensitive person, but for those they love and care about as well.

CHAPTER 14

Timing Is Everything

When problems arise, timing is everything, and everything is about timing. Wisely choosing the appropriate time to address an issue should be a number one priority. Doing so makes it easier for both parties to address, face, and resolve problems.

Few issues get resolved if you attempt to handle one issue while you are dealing with another—particularly, if they are unrelated. Thus, choosing the wrong time tends to make things worse. If an issue is to have any possibility of being resolved, it must be confronted at an appropriate time, which increases the likelihood that it will be resolved.

Certainly, the appropriate time is not when the atmosphere is already highly charged with negative emotions and/or you have not had enough time to think about the solution. Conversely, the best time for conflict resolution is when there are no other negative or heated issues being addressed, and, if at all possible, when both parties are relaxed.

Whenever you both are ready to discuss a problem or

issue, the chances of resolution increase. However, you may have difficulty trying to get some black men to agree to a time to discuss a problem, particularly when they feel they are in the wrong. If that is the case, you have to address the issue whenever you think the time is right.

When you do address an issue, you should have a solution in mind but be prepared to compromise. A good negotiating tip is to ask for more than you want and then be prepared to negotiate it down to no less than what is acceptable. Your man will be relieved, and you will be happy.

PART THREE

❄

Subduing the Games Men Play

CHAPTER 15

❄

One Game After Another

Taboo is what you would like to make it. But commonplace is what it is. I am referring to game playing or the games that black men play when communicating to you. This is an aspect of the black man's character that many black women detest. Maybe they dislike the games black men play because they are aware, through experience, hearsay, or observation, that it's a venture in which hearts are at stake. It's a game in which the loser often pays with tears, anger, and bitterness. It can be fun and joyous when you don't know what's ahead. But it can be demeaning and miserable when you finally find out. The rules and the boundaries are seldom well-defined. You may become a willing victim if he is a well-versed game player and you are innocent and naive. This obvious mismatch can create serious problems for you. Even hard work, if it's the wrong kind, can mean rejection as your payoff. The whole idea of game playing seems to violate the quality of a genuine relationship.

Yet, game playing is an intricate, important (yes, important), and often necessary part of the way black men communicate to you. Make no mistake about it! It is as much a part of their courting strategy as taking you to dinner and aiming to win your heart with flowers. Ironically, black men look for, want, and need women who can read, identify, and *reject* the games they play.

While the very thought of game playing can make many black women paranoid, attempting to find a man who does not play games can be slightly more difficult than finding that infamous needle in a haystack. With the right circumstances, any man is capable of playing games. Furthermore, the black man who tries *not* to play games is often boring to black women.

Now, if you were to ask black men if they play games with women, many would assuredly claim that they do not. They are aware that black women don't like to play games. But even black men who insist with all their heart that they don't play games do in fact play them unconsciously, if not consciously.

Indeed, you would be best served if you didn't take the games they play personally. Instead, assume that black men, from the simplest to the most sophisticated, can and will play games when they communicate with you.

In fact, when you get involved with a black man, you have positioned yourself for a game. You are one of the players, and you are playing a game whether you intend to or not. The best remedy is not to refuse to play (as many black women attempt to do), but to identify and understand the objective of his games, as I will clarify here. When you demystify the game, you demystify the man.

Black men grow up learning and playing games with black women. Game playing is one way they control relationships. Thus, some men would say, "The better my game, the more control I have." Many learn to equate the quality of their game with the quality of their manhood. Therefore, if they are smooth or have a good game, they think they should be able to demonstrate their ability with either the type or the number of women they can get.

There is little doubt that when you can't play a black man's game you will not get quality commitment from him. Plus, it is very likely that you're on a path to losing the commitment you already have. Doing all you can to make a relationship work probably won't do you any good if you don't understand how to avoid the problems that his game playing creates.

On the other hand, no matter how good a black man thinks his game is, when a woman knows his game and can put him in check properly, he responds very positively. Not only is he inclined to give quality commitment, but his love and respect are likely to increase as well.

Despite the many negative connotations game playing carries, it unfortunately has become an important means of communication for black men. Note that while the games that black men play may vary substantially, their objective is often the same. The use of game playing serves several purposes. When "rapping" or attempting to establish relationships, black men can find a great deal of security in game playing. It helps them to pursue women and, if necessary, to deal with rejection more easily. For example, if you reject a black man's advances, game playing allows him more room to respond than if he were just serious and straightforward. This helps him to protect his ego and his heart. Ultimately, he can use game playing to play the whole situation off, as if he meant nothing serious by what he said or did. Yet, he is well aware that the payoff for game playing could be the woman he's after.

Sometimes black men use game playing to show affection, but they use it far more often to avoid commitment and to avoid falling in love. They rely on it most handily when they are being unfaithful or are planning to be. Furthermore, black men not only play games to start relationships but also to end them.

You might be surprised to know that among the various ways a black man uses game playing, one of the most important is to evaluate you. He uses it to determine what kind of relationship you and he will have.

The man you are communicating to might not give any indication that he's a game player, but you would still be better off to assume that, like other men, he is. Black women are quick to cut off those black men who have obvious games. Ironically, that has forced some black men to make their games more subtle. Thus, the best game players are not obvious.

This doesn't mean you have to be paranoid, but rather

that you should monitor your relationships and keep an eye out, right from the start, for the games men play. All too often in a new relationship, when you find out he's "running a game" and don't do anything about it, you have already given him what he wanted but not what he's looking for. I reiterate, a black man looks for and commits to a woman who is able to stop his game playing. If you don't stop him, his game playing will hinder intimacy and/or prevent genuine companionship.

I am reminded of Zelda, a friend who called to tell me she had met the perfect man. He was interested in her, not himself. He wrote poetry, they went on walks, they spent time in the library, and sex was not his primary concern. As I quizzed her about the man, there were too many questions she couldn't answer. But believing him to be honest and decent, she made the mistake of going to bed with him. While she was expecting more love, she found out that there was more to the man than he had initially revealed. He had a woman with children, and no intention of ending that relationship.

The "Good Guy Game"

Zelda was a victim of the "Good Guy Game," or GGG. GGG is when a man comes into your life and appears to be a good person. You enjoy his company, and he is not totally focused on taking you to bed. He's a breath of fresh air compared to many of the other black men you have dated. So you relax, put down your guard, and then discover, usually after you have gone to bed with him, that he's not much different from the rest.

The inherent problem is that you gave him what he wanted and not what he was looking for. But the truth is, if he is really a good guy and not a fake, he can and will wait as you cultivate a balanced relationship and get real commitment.

In a loving, established relationship, most black men don't play games on an ongoing basis. If they do play them, they usually wait for the appropriate time. Temptation and lust can sometimes make a black man feel that the time is appropriate to play games, and this can get a good man to initiate a bad game. It is because of the way black men are oriented to their sexuality that oftentimes they haven't developed the morals or willpower to control their sex drive. It's no excuse, but it's true. Many of them need a woman who can recognize when they start to play games so that they won't do wrong. This doesn't mean that a woman has to watch a man's every step. In fact, if a woman cuts his game short, he is more likely to monitor himself out of respect for her ability to recognize and challenge his behavior. The woman who can recognize the signs of game playing and address them early can avoid unnecessary pain and problems in her relationship.

The "Monogamous Game"

In some relationships, particularly a new or developing one, black men will initiate the "Monogamous Game" to see if you are the type of person who will take a solid stand about monogamy. He might joke about being with other women or suggest that it takes more than one woman to satisfy him. What's important to him in this little game is your reaction to his statements. What he determines from monitoring and evaluating your reaction will likely determine his future course of action.

Not only does this unscrupulous game tell him what you won't tolerate, but it also gives him an idea of what he can get away with in a relationship with you. The best response is to stop him the moment you recognize the game. You don't have to get loud or ugly. You need only let him know, in a friendly but no-nonsense way, that you don't tolerate infidelity. The more firmly you send the message, the less likely he will follow through with the reality of this game.

In the "Monogamous Game," if you aren't able to take a strong stance, in all likelihood you can forget about quality commitment. Sooner or later he will find trouble, or he will not have the willpower to say no should trouble find him.

On her first date with Tony, Sheila didn't wait for him to play the "Monogamous Game." In the course of their conversation, she told him that she would only accept a monogamous relationship. There was no middle ground. Tony knew that she was serious. There was no need for him to play the "Monogamous Game" because she had already made her position clear. At that point, Sheila didn't mind losing Tony, and he knew how he had to behave if he wanted to maintain a relationship with her.

Still, in a seasoned relationship, one in which a man is committed, he might check to see if his woman has weakened her stance on the monogamous issue. It's not uncommon for some women to start out with strong convictions and then make the mistake of acting less concerned as long as he returns home. A woman in this position usually fears losing her man if she speaks up or challenges his actions. She fails to realize that speaking up is often what it takes to keep a relationship monogamous.

The "Don't Check on Me Game"

Next there is the "Don't Check on Me Game." In this situation, a man is asserting his right not to be checked on. He feels that he should be trusted, and he is right. There is little need to check on a man who loves you as much as you love him, or more.

If you feel you have to check up on him, you may be in the middle of a game. The very motive for him saying "don't check up on me" may be to see what boundaries and guidelines he can get you to accept in the name of trust, fairness, love—or maybe even indignation.

On the one hand, his position may seem fair, valid, and prideful. A man may need his space, and you shouldn't be afraid to give it to him. On the other hand, if there is nothing to hide, there is no need to establish strict guidelines. You should make that point known and then assure him that if there are any guidelines established, the two of you should have substantial input and come to a mutual agreement. The bottom line is that if you play this game, you should play it with rules and terms you can handle, or you'll end up playing at a disadvantage—causing you to lose the game.

The "Blame Game"

Next there is the "Blame Game." This is a game in which a black man gets a woman to accept his problems by blaming his predicament on his mother, or more likely on a woman from a previous relationship. For example, he might say he can't commit, or he can't hold hands, or he can't love because the woman in his past relationship did him wrong. In reality, the "Blame Game" is his way of saying, "I'm not going to give you a complete relationship." He'll use the problems from his past as his ultimate excuse.

But like the other games, black men play the "Blame

Game" only with women who are willing to play it. He knows that he is not responsible for your past mistakes and that you are not responsible for his. You accept a burden and a hindrance to a complete relationship when you allow him to bring unnecessary baggage from his past relationships.

Right or wrong, one of the things that the black male sexual image suggests is that a man has to be strong enough to handle the downs of love. That belief can actually help a man to get a grip and go on from a failed relationship—unless he finds a new woman who will allow him to use excuses about his past to avoid moving forward and establishing a genuine relationship with her.

A further extension of the "Blame Game" occurs when he consistently blames his negative behavior on his parents or the way he was raised. A man who respects a woman and realizes that he can't play such games on her will adopt new behavior almost instantly. It is a good idea not to accept "Blame Game" excuses. Let him know that you don't want to play the "Blame Game" because the two of you can blame others for any behavior you don't want to change. If he insists on blaming others for things that hinder your relationship or to excuse his negative behavior, you should deal with it until you get the desired change. Otherwise, it can cripple your relationship.

The "I'm So Jealous Game"

Then there is the "I'm So Jealous I Can't Help Myself Game." His jealousy could be real, but only put up with it when he's also showing you love and respect. Some men use jealousy to manipulate women. Once a man gets you to play this game, not only can he get on your nerves, but he can take you through many changes. This game can also become dangerous, so, if possible, nip it in the bud. Tell him that you don't want to play this game and get his agreement not to play! If necessary, describe his behavior to him. Ask him what message he intends to communicate with his actions. Then let him know what messages you receive from his behavior. Follow through by telling him the best way he can make his point to you. Making some men aware of the games they play will get them to stop playing them, but others have to be continually put in check the moment they start to play.

The difference between this game and the "Green-Eyed Monster" is that the "I'm So Jealous Game" is used to control you. In the "Green-Eyed Monster," you are in control, using the power of jealousy to enhance your relationship.

The "Evaluation Game"

Game playing allows black men to see how much of a lady you are, how vulnerable you would be to games that other men play, and how much respect you demand. If you appear to be a weak woman (one who can't stop his game playing), he will know that very early in your relationship. It is from that information that he will determine if he can have you, run his game, and have other women too.

Game playing also allows him to see how confident and secure you are as a person. If you are insecure, you probably will not effectively challenge the games he plays. Given the confusion that a game can create, you might convince yourself that you don't understand what he's doing, or you might not try to understand. Then it will not be long before you start to accept his deviant and sometimes ugly behavior. You will also discover that the more game playing you accept from him, the less confidence you will eventually have in your relationship as well as in yourself. Also, it's not likely that he will stop playing games until he is finished with you.

In the meantime, you will probably find yourself in an unhappy relationship, hoping that he will change, but accepting a shadow of a relationship as your true destiny and love in life.

The fact is, he won't give you quality commitment because he knows he doesn't have to. He realizes he can have you as long as you remain subject to his game. It is a case of "if you have the cow, why pay for the milk?"

Even in a seasoned relationship, some men will, from time to time, consistently try to run their game on the woman in their life. If she wants to avoid problems, she has to meet the challenge. It might be just what he needs to stay committed. It's usually a mistake to let a black man run his game on you out of love or insecurity.

Furthermore, your love for him and/or your insecurities about the relationship can cause you to become very passive. Silence is not an effective way to deal with game playing. If your man is playing a game with you, and you respond with silence, you are indicating that you have not acknowledged that a game is being played. If he continues to run his game, your passiveness only makes things worse for you and better for him to play his game.

The most effective way to handle game playing is to remain calm and firm, address the game, and refuse to play. Whenever possible, nip it in the bud. Remember, too, that whenever you start to get confused on any issue because of the message you get from him, calmly and firmly, in a respectful, no-nonsense kind of way, address the issue as soon as appropriate. The appropriate time can be decided by you or agreed upon between the two of you. But ensure that it is a time when no other issues (especially potentially negative ones) are being addressed.

The Nature of Games

Be advised that much of what black men say and do is behavior that reflects the influence of the black male sexual image, and oftentimes it is second nature. Therefore, it is not uncommon for some black men to be unaware of the games they play.

A change in a black man's attitude or behavior is often an indication that a game has begun. If not, good! But if you find yourself involved in a game, there is no need to panic, get upset and angry, get loud, or become overly aggressive. Indeed, you should do just the opposite. Become calm. The greater his game, the greater your calmness and seriousness should be.

Be aware that if you love him more than he loves you, your Love Scale is out of balance, and not only are you in a game, but you are losing. Another indication of your being in a game and losing is that you have had sex with him and felt it was inappropriate, and/or you are confused about how you let it go so far.

Finally, if you are not able to please him with most of what you do, it's often an indication that he may be attempting to end the relationship, or that he's seeing or pursuing another woman. Of course, there's always the possibility that he's just dissatisfied in general.

In some cases, your man's loss of love may be so great that when you attempt to restore balance by stopping his game, he will want out. His game playing may be the only thing keeping him in the relationship. If that is the case, you're probably in a dictatorship and not a relationship. Communication should be based on your terms as well as his. Get a grip. If you are unhappy, it may be better for you to leave him or end the relationship.

It does not matter how good a woman you are; when a man is aware that he can run his game on you, he perceives you as weak. Some women make the mistake of believing that all they have to be is a good woman and that a man will see how valuable they are, have mercy, and not run his game on them. Wrong! Good women are often more of a target because they don't have a hidden agenda, or their goodness is, for the most part, all that's needed for a man to feel comfortable about playing a game. All the things you have done for him and the hard work you have put into the relationship may not matter. You yourself may know of women who were good to their men, yet their men played games with them anyway.

Clearly, if a man is willing to play his game and let a "good" woman go, there must be strong reasons for such actions. When you understand those reasons, you are not only in a position to demystify his game, but to him you are demonstrating a sense of strength and intelligence. You also avoid a game being played on you, and ultimately you increase your chances of maintaining a healthy relationship.

Remember, even good men can have bad games. Take a game player and turn him into a dedicated family man.

Only when you have effectively dealt with his game playing will he be in a frame of mind to commit. Ultimately, you should end up with a good man who's *really* good.

CHAPTER 16

❄

Undecipherable Communication

When a black man makes confusion his ally, it's usually your enemy. Being confused about what a man means by what he says and does might seem normal in any given relationship. But with black men, it's a good chance that what appears to be normal can help him do abnormal things.

You could be facing a style of communication that black men quietly rely on. If he is just getting to know you and discovers that you won't confront and/or stop this style of communication, he probably will not see a need to make a true commitment to you, if any commitment at all. However, if he does commit and you don't recognize and stop this style of communication, it is very likely that you are already in—or are about to be involved in—an unhappy relationship.

Although this pattern of sometimes subtle but always undecipherable communication is more likely to happen in a new relationship, it can occur at *any* point in a relationship. Even women in seasoned relationships can suddenly find themselves facing undecipherable communication. Once this problem gets started, it could easily get worse before it gets better if you don't effectively confront it.

For many black men there is a "natural" tendency to communicate in a confusing manner. Many aren't even consciously aware that it is taking place, but they still do it. It's natural in that it is one way they define the nature of their relationship with you: leaving undecipherable communication for you to clear up. Don't base your relationship with a man on unclear messages. If you do, it could be the beginning of relationship troubles.

You know you have a problem in this area when you simply don't understand his words and/or his behavior. You may just be slightly puzzled and confused, or you may not have a clue as to what he means. He could have you puzzled with slang or plain English. Your first reaction might be to ask a friend, his or yours, what he means. Since you don't understand his words and/or his actions, the entire ordeal can be frustrating. Yet, being frustrated and showing it is often the worst of all possible responses. Furthermore, you may have already discovered that frustration is not likely to elicit the understanding or sympathy you crave.

Undecipherable communication is simply not an asset to your relationship. But like some of the other issues we have discussed, if the man you are communicating to is using it or is attempting to use it, you have it within your power to stop him and avoid a problematic and potentially disastrous relationship.

Making your man clarify his communication serves several purposes. Not only does it force him to continually define the relationship in a clear way, but it also reflects how much respect you require. If he does not know you very well, he will test you to see how you react. Some of the things he tries might even be put in a joking context, but he still reads your reactions. If he can get away with communicating to you with what amounts to jive, bull, baffle, and/or nonsensical communication, you become a prime candidate for the disrespectful games he can play.

An illustration of this can be seen in Andrea's relationship with Cliff. They had been dating for two months when she admitted that she liked him a great deal. Andrea's problem with Cliff was that he had her home phone number, whereas the only place she could contact him was at work. She had asked for his number, but he had managed to give her undecipherable communication instead. In effect, she really didn't know why she didn't have his home number. Once he found that he could get away with this, Cliff waited until Andrea's heart was involved in their relationship before revealing that he lived with another woman and was expected to marry her. Still, Andrea accepted his living arrangements because Cliff said something about leaving that relationship for her. Even then, Andrea couldn't say exactly when Cliff was planning to leave, or what he meant by his statement.

She had accepted more babble. When it was over, Andrea was left with what she accepted from Cliff—undecipherable communication and no Cliff.

When a black man learns that he can tell a woman anything, sooner or later that's exactly what he'll tell her—*anything*! Since there is a "natural" tendency for black men to take you through this process, even a black man who wants to respect you is going to have a difficult time doing so if you are a woman who will accept babble.

Andrea is not alone. There are many women who are involved with black men but know very little about them because what they know is based on those men's undecipherable communication. The women may have even asked some questions, and the men may have given them some answers. Their responses, however, often leave black women confused or with a nebulous impression— an impression that's flexible enough to allow the men to reshape the meaning if and when necessary. This can keep you from being sure about some very key issues in a man's life—particularly when what he is explaining has something to do with a woman who was or is in his life. His first attempt to explain this may very well be undecipherable communication. His subsequent explanations will usually be based on how you accept the first round of babble.

Black men use undecipherable communication to determine if they are going to establish a substantive relationship with a woman. When they are looking for a companion, they will use it to help determine whether or not she is a serious candidate. Should you not have what it takes to warmly confront a man when he uses undecipherable communication, he may silently conclude that you are someone he can dupe or get over on, and that you may not be quite woman enough for him.

What he will consciously or unconsciously realize is that while dating you, should he choose, he can see other women and rely on undecipherable communication if you confront him. On the other hand, he may have significant feelings for you and be honestly trying to avoid temptation. But should the temptation become too great, his relationship with you will not be a deterrent. He will likely conclude that he can succumb to the temptation and respond to you with babble later. Remember, such behavior is either more strongly influenced by his understanding of the black male sexual image or by his love and respect for you. Oftentimes, the more black men can get away with by using undecipherable communication, the more often they will use it.

Moreover, it seems that everyone else can decipher a man's so-called undecipherable communication except the woman involved. When she discusses it with someone, she's likely to hear that the man is probably messing around with other women. What she doesn't usually hear is that she could possibly have avoided this negative situation had she effectively dealt with his undecipherable communication pattern in the first place.

The foremost thing that you can and should do is recognize undecipherable communication for what it is. You should know if a man has already lowered you, or is attempting to lower you, into an undecipherable communication pattern. What you want is clear, logical, and make-sense communication.

You should never let him put you in a position where you are consistently playing a guessing game or trying to figure out what he's doing, where he is, or what he means by what he says. Your guessing may become a weak substitute for two-way communication and getting him to stop the babble.

The pattern of undecipherable communication can occur at any point in your relationship. A man in a seasoned marriage will use it when he is faced with temptation he doesn't want to resist. When his wife attempts to find out why his behavior has abruptly changed, he is likely to give her a response embedded with confusion. What he says may not make any sense, but, like many black men, he may use anger and irritation to fortify his position and ensure that his woman doesn't challenge him or ask too many questions.

Adell knew that Drew was not thrilled about his job. In fact, he seldom did overtime. In the last two months, however, he was doing overtime without complaining. When she asked him why he was suddenly so willing to do overtime, he became very defensive. Instead of responding to her question, he accused her of interfering with his basic right and need to earn a living. He became so disturbed that she chose to be silent. Not too long after that, in the midst of the confusion he had created, she suddenly realized that he was having an affair.

Once a black man subjects you to undecipherable communication, it is likely that things will get worse before they get better if you don't effectively challenge him. The undecipherable communication pattern could easily be the disease that makes for an unhappy relationship and eventually destroys it.

Despite everything I've already said, be aware that there are times when a man may appear to be using undecipherable communication, but he's not necessarily up to no good. He may simply not be communicating clearly, or you may just misunderstand him. You will have to decide which is the case and respond accordingly.

If undecipherable communication has managed to become part of a man's communication pattern for some time, his reaction to your challenge for change might be compared to that of an untamed horse. He will do quite a bit to throw you off, but if you stay properly focused on the problem, he will calm down and respect your desire. Just realize that some men will test you and attempt to pull you into a cycle of undecipherable communication with anger, jokes, silence, threats, intimidation, and, in the worst cases, physical harm. They will declare a subject off-limits, pretend they have no idea what you're talking about, or make you think that you are at fault for their actions and are creating a problem simply for bringing a subject up. Some will go so far as to say that they did what they did because you accused them of doing it. There is no limit to what some black men can think of to lower you into accepting babble so that they can avoid genuine communication.

You should avoid physical confrontation at all cost. If necessary, you can be firm and serious and still not be overly argumentative or confrontational.

The most effective way to deal with undecipherable communication is to avoid being frustrated by it. Frustration is a sign that he has you off balance and possibly poised for defeat. If you know that he is trying to lower you into an undecipherable communication pattern, recognize it and smile inside. Rule Number One: When you ask a question, calmly and firmly, in a respectful, nononsense kind of way, stay focused on the primary issue. Rule Number Two: If he still does not make sense or if you are simply confused, refer back to Rule Number One. Nothing satisfies you like a clear answer. It's that simple.

There will be times when you will get a great deal of respect from a man just by challenging his undecipherable communication. Your ultimate reward will be that the communication lines will be clearer and more open and honest. Thus, while he will be less inclined to play games with your heart, he will also be more likely to rate you higher on the Love Scale. The bottom line is that you will definitely have a happier relationship.

CHAPTER 17

❄

Fronting

Julia boldly ordered a full-course meal and a very nice glass of wine while secretly knowing he wanted her to order hors d'oeuvres only.

Now he was opening her door as she eased into his sleek, stylish Mercedes. He didn't know that she would make this their first and last date.

The day they met, he gave her his business card because he wanted her to know that he was a lawyer. Julia thought she had a great catch. But a few days later, she discovered that he was the same lawyer who had been engaged to one of her best girlfriends. Suddenly, she knew more about him than his business card would ever tell.

During dinner, he glamorized his work and exaggerated his status. She knew that he was working out of his house, just barely able to make the payments on his car, and that he really couldn't afford to pay for dinner, not to mention the wine.

As he drove her home, he was expecting more, and he received it. She bluntly told him that she didn't date her friend's ex-men and then revealed that she knew all about him. He became fiercely upset, not only because she had inside information, but also because she waited until the end of the date to tell him.

In her mind, Julia was making him pay for fronting—acting as if he had it all together and trying to appear to be someone he wasn't: a successful lawyer. She wanted him to pay for fronting because she knew that the average woman would have been swept off her feet, believing that with his front, he was about more than what he was.

Naturally, a black man, like any man, wants to impress the woman he communicates to. He wants to at least impress a woman enough to influence her perception in order to gain her acceptance. Consequently, many black men go to extreme lengths to give women the impression that they have it all together when they in fact do not. They are fronting. Like the lawyer, many are hoping that by the time a woman realizes that they are fronting, she will have given them what they want. Certainly, if you give a black man what he's looking for rather than what he wants, the quality of your communication will go far beyond fronting.

A black man goes through so much just to survive that when he is successful on top of that, his success is often a pleasant surprise. If he's also single, then many black women will see him as a desired and rare GEM (Good Ebony Man). When black women check out black men, they look for signs that he's a GEM. Unsurprisingly, it's those same signs that some black men use as a front to give the appearance that they are GEMs.

A nice car, a nice suit, a nice pair of shoes, and a business card are the four primary tools for fronting. Black men realize that many black women make the mistake of looking for these as signs of success. Many black women believe that having those four fronting tools makes a statement, at the very least, about a black man's current status. Maybe to some degree these things do say something about the man, but not enough to draw a true or even an intelligent conclusion about him or what he has accomplished.

Black men who have little or nothing going for them can acquire the tools for fronting, and in the process get what they want from black women. Some black men even boast that fronting with all four of the tools can be so effective that when they have them, they can often get more women than they can handle. That is in part why I sound the alarm so loudly. As long as they are successful with this technique, black men are going to front. To prevent unnecessary problems, black women should position themselves to get past a man's front and see who he really is and what he's really about. The intention is not to embarrass a black man or put him down, but to guide your relationship to a healthier course.

Not all men who front use only the most obvious tools. Some use houses, yachts, bank accounts, cruises, and so on. Similarly, not all black men who front have negative intentions. Many use it as a way to attract women so that they can then develop a more substantive relationship. Quite frankly, if they didn't have a front, they would probably attract far fewer women.

The problem is not that fronting works, but that it can negatively affect some potentially good relationships. Fronting starts a relationship off on false pretenses, when in fact most people are looking for true substantial relationships. Because fronting is pretending, it can have people wasting time trying to cover things up. In an attempt to maintain a good front, some black men take their relationship through many unnecessary changes. It causes them to make promises they can't keep, to distort the truth, and to outright lie.

Vanessa was engaged and practically married to Derrick when she found out that his Lexus was not in the shop waiting for a part to arrive from overseas, because he didn't even own a Lexus. Furthermore, like other men who front, he had taken her to upscale places that suggested he was in a certain income bracket. Derrick had long wanted to tell Vanessa that he had lied about the car and was pretending to be more than he really was, but he just couldn't bring himself to do it for fear of losing her.

To be duped by a man's fronting may be an indication that you are focusing on the outer edges of who he is. Never talk yourself into thinking you know a man when all you really know is his front.

Most black men would probably agree that if they had

to have only one of the fronting tools to impress women, their choice would be a nice car. This is one reason why black men put so much emphasis on cars.

Some black men believe that their car communicates or raps to women for them, while all they have to do is look as good as they possibly can. Black men tell many stories of women that they were able to date because they were in the right type of car.

Keith, for example, was having a tough time getting a date while driving an older model Ford. He got a temporary sales job and was fortunate enough to close several sizable transactions, which allowed him to buy a new Mercedes, even with bad credit. Keith literally didn't own a good blanket for his bed, but he was riding around in high style. Almost instantly, he had his datebook filled. Women who would have refused to give him the time of day were now deeming him legitimate and giving him their bodies. Women who were otherwise intelligent didn't seem to realize that they were trading themselves for a ride and maybe a chance to be seen in Keith's car. (Note that Keith and the women he dated were over thirty.)

To make matters worse, too much success with fronting often keeps many black men from striving toward real success. It becomes a security blanket. They are aware that having all or some of the tools for fronting is likely to give them easier access to black women. They often stay in relationships hiding behind their fronts. By the time a woman discovers that the man is all front and nothing else, she is often deeply involved. If she then presses him to develop his potential, he may be too insecure and choose to take his fronting act to another woman. That's when you hear black women saying, "Honey, let him go ahead. She can have him." Then he'll probably stay with the new woman until she demands more and he leaves again. And so the cycle continues.

Meeting a black man who does nothing but front can be like going to a Hollywood set where you are impressed by the magnificent facade of a house and then discover that there's nothing behind it—no bedroom, kitchen, or bathroom, and definitely no family room; just a few props holding it up.

The truth is, many of those black men out there fronting have plenty of potential, and potential is a good quality to look for in a black man. Take the lawyer, for instance. He could have been honest and up front about his current situation. It would have given him a better opportunity to see if Julia wanted to know him or what he had to offer her at the moment. He could have avoided spending more on that date than he could afford. Similarly, Julia could have taken the time to check out his potential (which could be negative, although he's a lawyer) as well as his inner qualities, which should be of primary concern. If he has some potential and the right inner qualities, everything else can follow. A woman who is attracted to a man who has all the tools for fronting, including an excellent job, but possesses negative inner qualities may experience an absolute nightmare. This is something that black women should remember who say, "He must have a good job."

Even if you are not one of those women who are easily moved by the obvious tools of fronting, you may still have to confront and deal with a black man who has a front. As I mentioned, not all black men who front have bad intentions.

Black men will often resort to the confusion game to keep you from getting past their front.

Always check to see if the man you are communicating to is pretending to be something he is not. Don't let his fronting deceive you. It's one of the most overused and oldest games around. Con artists use the same tools to influence your perception that men use who front. The primary difference is intention. A con artist intends to get from you what he can, usually while giving up as little as possible. His front is often a part of his con; it's usually very difficult to discover who the man behind the con really is. The black man who is simply fronting is more interested in you than the con artist is. However, the thing to remember is that both will usually resort to the confusion game to keep you from getting past their front. You will know that a man is succeeding at this game when you are confused about things that you should be clear on.

Some men stop fronting when they realize that you are truly more interested in them than in what they own.

There are black men who use fronting simply as a means of attracting the women they are interested in. If you discover that a man was fronting and he has no Mercedes or little of anything else, but he does have (1) *positive inner qualities*, which means he respects and treats you right, and (2) *potential*, which means he's confident and has goals that he's working diligently toward—take him home and do so proudly.

CHAPTER 18

❄

Secret Relationships

Hiding your relationship with a man from other people is sometimes the best thing you can do in order to peacefully establish a strong foundation. Furthermore, sometimes prematurely announcing that you are in a relationship or contending that you have more than what you do can lead to problems, pain, and embarrassment if things don't work out. There is a tendency for many of us to inflate a disagreement or breakup, depending on how many people know about the situation.

At any rate, it's not unusual to start a relationship in secrecy. But when you are a man's secret and his sexship, you will likely have problems and maybe even regret it if you ever decide you want greater commitment and a more ideal relationship.

Being a black man's secret is not a good idea when you want and deserve more. Yet, not only can it happen deliberately, it can easily happen unintentionally.

Rita and Lucas started out their relationship with the intention of keeping it private from everyone except a few select people. They had many friends in common and thought this plan would be best, since they were not sure if things would work out. But after more than a year of dating, even Lucas had to admit that they were in more than a casual relationship.

During that year, Rita had met Lucas's parents and the rest of his family. But what appeared significant really was not. Women are often deceived by meeting a man's family. While that can be a good sign of his interest, it might not mean anything.

Meanwhile, Rita began to increasingly feel that all the secrecy was no longer necessary. Aside from his family members, only Lucas's best friend knew about them. The rest of his friends, particularly the females, saw him as an available single man—a perception that can bring its own set of problems. Not only did Rita want to put an end to that, but in her heart she wanted her relationship with Lucas to be publicly acknowledged.

You are probably in a secret relationship if you don't know a man's family or friends very well or those people who are important to him. But the best sign of a secret relationship is that he ensures that other women don't know about you.

Lloyd had been dating Sonia for six months. At first, she didn't think that she had a secret relationship with him. After all, she had met his mother and a few of his friends. Furthermore, whenever she took him to meet people that she knew, he had no problem letting them see that he had a close relationship with her. But then she began to notice that when he took *her* places, particularly where there were other women, he acted as if they were nothing more than casual friends. Ordinarily, that would have been fine with her, because she didn't especially need public demonstrations of his affection. However, this remoteness when they were with *his* friends was too obvious.

If you think that you're in a secret relationship, you are not alone. Such relationships can be fairly common among black men. A secret relationship is usually not about him being ashamed of you, as some women tend to believe. Rather, it's about him having the advantage of appearing single or at least available. By not going public, it offers him the perfect opportunity for multiple relationships. Thus, you should avoid secret relationships unless they fit your needs.

Even when a good relationship starts to go sour, one of the first things that many men do is ensure that what is left becomes a secret relationship. If a man appears unattached, he can make a smoother transition to another woman. Quite often, this is also the time when the woman he is leaving is waiting for him to say the words "it's over" to make it official—instead of seeing that his *actions* are saying, "it's over." Thus, she finds herself in a secret sexship, prolonging the inevitable.

When some black women find themselves in secret relationships, they make the mistake of trying to force the relationship public. They want and insist that the man take them places so that they can be seen together. What they fail to realize is that black men resent and resist being forced to take a relationship public, particularly if they have had a secret relationship with a woman for a considerable amount of time.

If you have to pressure a black man to be seen with you in public, you need to realize that there are other issues, such as those discussed in previous chapters, that need to be addressed. Insisting that others know about you and your man will not necessarily enhance the quality of the relationship.

In some cases, it is not unusual for a woman's pressure to cause a man to abruptly end their relationship. In doing so, he may be bluffing or he may be sincere. But either way, he probably wants to keep himself available for other women.

There are several positive reasons why black men will voluntarily take a relationship out of secrecy. Most do so out of increased love and respect for a woman. Usually, this also indicates that they are willing to make more of a commitment. It could be said that the more public a man is willing to take a relationship, the greater the commitment he is willing to make. However, going public might not mean a thing. Many a black man will let the world know that a woman is his, while continuing to do whatever he desires—a clear indication of her weak position in the relationship.

However, whether your relationship is weak or strong,

you should avoid creating a secret relationship unless it meets *your* needs. In any case, you should avoid being a black man's secret sexship even if it means letting him go forever.

CHAPTER 19

❄

Mr. Crazy

Crazy is how he is consistently described. This is not a guy who's called crazy because he does funny and outlandish things. The man I'm referring to has a quick temper and goes off on emotional tantrums. He's often overly sensitive and unpredictable. Little things can upset him. Many of your friends don't like to be around him. They, like many of his own family members, say he's crazy. Some say that *you* are the crazy one for staying in a relationship with him. But you feel you know him better than they do.

After all, you know his quiet, loving, intimate side. To you he's only half-crazy or a little crazy or not crazy at all. Nevertheless, deep down, because people call him crazy, you are sometimes intimidated by him. However, you know he only acts that way at times. You might have even learned what ticks him off and, for the most part, avoid saying or doing those things.

In addition, when he has one of his tantrums and you feel violated emotionally or otherwise, it can be difficult for you to get quality support from family and friends.

After all, they have already told you to leave him. Plus, every time he does something negative, the less patience they have and the more they dislike him. In many cases, they can't even stand to hear about him. Still, with all that, you feel he's not as bad as they believe he is, although there are moments when you think you could be fooling yourself.

There are some black men who like the label of being called crazy, and probably have earned it. These men do what they can to live up to the billing, and for this reason probably *are* crazy. I have not met a woman yet who says she desires a crazy man, and neither should you.

However, many black men are *not* crazy, they just *act* crazy. It's often learned behavior. Go into any given home with children and you will see them having fits or tantrums so that they can have their way. You will see parents giving them what they want so that they will be quiet. These parents don't realize that their children are learning how to ask for things with negative behavior. It's either cute or too much for parents to deal with. But when these children are still screaming and having tantrums when they're adults, then they're labeled crazy.

I have seen mothers who allowed their sons to grow up without discipline or respect for black women. Then, when the boys become men, the mothers will often attempt to compensate for their sons' shortcomings by doing such things as paying off their loans, making excuses for their lack of discipline, or warning their girlfriends that the sons are no good.

In fact, a man may be no good, but that doesn't necessarily mean he's crazy. What he is doing with his crazy behavior is using a form of communication that he has become comfortable with to get his way. And he'll get his way with *you* if you let him.

Melba had been dating Fred for seven months when they had their first major disagreement. He stood over her as if he were about to hit her. He screamed at the top of his lungs and showed no sense of being reasonable. He would not let her talk. Fred was into his "I'm crazy" act. He had shown her a couple of little signs before, but nothing like this one. Melba was frightened and decided to remain calm and quiet. When she got home, she called him and told him that their relationship was over. Fred did what he could to restore the relationship, but Melba would not allow it. Fred was not crazy. He was the one who told me how he had lost Melba by trying to control her the way he had controlled other women in the past— by *playing* crazy.

Many black men play crazy in their relationships because they realize it's a label that society in general and blacks in particular will readily accept about them. Consequently, many black men adapt a "crazy personality" to control people around them.

Black pimps often play crazy, not only in their movie roles but in reality as well, to get women to do what they want. Many black men have picked up on this, consciously or unconsciously, and brought the behavior into their own relationships.

However, some black men are extremely convincing at playing crazy. They may use a prior brush with the law, or time in prison, or some act of violence to help make their "playing crazy" more believable. Unfortunately, a few of these men start to believe their own hype, motivated by their fears and insecurities and probably wishing they knew a better way to communicate.

Monya's man Leo played craziness to the hilt. Monya's family and friends all said he was a "crazy man," although not literally crazy, and that she was a crazy woman for staying with him. Playing crazy allowed Leo to take advantage of Monya financially and psychologically.

Because Leo was thought to be crazy, whenever a man called Monya on the phone, even on a business matter, Leo acted as if he couldn't understand it. At the same time, he had women friends who could call him whenever they pleased. When Monya and Leo agreed to end their relationship and to see other people, but to continue living in the same house, she lived in fear while he enjoyed himself.

One day when Leo saw Monya with another man who happened to be much smaller than Leo, he went into his "I'm crazy" act. He put her under house arrest, ripped his shirt open so that his muscles could be seen, and then proceeded to tear up stuff in the house and throw furniture around. All this behavior was consistent with the idea that

Leo was supposed to be crazy. He created such a scene that Monya finally wanted out.

When she left, Leo apologized for his behavior, cried, and asked her to come back home. It was too late. Her departure was permanent. As terrible and crazy as he acted, Leo is not and never was crazy. He is in fact an otherwise intelligent man who tried to use playing crazy as a means to manage and control the people he knew intimately. When this approach eventually failed, he tried to show that he was not crazy, but it was too late.

Those black men who are not really crazy usually are smart enough to pick the right people and the right places to have their tantrums. Very often, black men who act crazy only do so around their partners, family members, and friends, knowing they can do so safely. Most stop the crazy act the moment two white policemen show up. Moreover, there is usually at least one family member with whom they know not to play crazy. That doesn't mean that there will not be times when they might misjudge and pick the wrong moment to go off. But such moments don't happen often. Occasionally, the men might choose to go crazy in an unusual setting. But then they are well aware that doing so adds creditability to their act.

If a so-called "crazy" man is employed, usually he knows how far to take his "crazy" attitude on the job, because he's not really crazy. Seldom will he go off on bigger, stronger-looking black men that he doesn't know.

(Playing crazy is an act, not a foolish talent.) Often crazy-acting men are physically big, having learned that their bigness helps them to get away with the act. Sometimes the bigger a man is, the more willing people are to believe that he's actually crazy.

The use of drugs can make people literally crazy or unstable. However, some black men use alcohol and other drugs as excuses to go into their "crazy" act. Still, it seems that certain people can stop the so-called crazy black man from going into a state of craziness. It's usually people, including women, he respects who won't tolerate such behavior.

Black men can play crazy in one relationship and not dare do it in another. Usually this is because he knows that certain women will surely leave him if he displays such negative and childish behavior. (He also may not play crazy because she has too many brothers.) However, if he doesn't have people in his life that he respects, that's indication enough to let him have his crazy world all to himself.

Should you find yourself in a relationship with a man who plays crazy, don't confirm and approve his behavior by referring to him as "half-crazy"—or any other kind of crazy, for that matter. Instead, point out what he has done and ask him not to play crazy again. If he is willing to change his behavior, suggest to him a better way to communicate his feelings. It is, of course, best to discuss this when he's acting sensible. Even so, some men will go into their "crazy" act the moment you bring up the subject. Therefore, your safety must always remain the number one priority. If necessary, and if at all possible, be willing to seek professional help.

Most important of all, you should *never* accept responsibility for the behavior of a black man who plays crazy. Don't let him get you to believe his behavior is your fault. It's his act, and he owns it all.

Black men who play crazy often take it too far and hurt the people around them. Then later they want you to accept their excuses and apologies. Playing crazy can be a dangerous game. If he doesn't recognize what he's doing and take responsibility for it, you should reconsider your relationship with him for the sake of your own safety.

Certainly, the time to reconsider your relationship with a man is when you think he has a problem, and he doesn't think so. If he is abusive in any way, or if your love is interrupted with periods of fear or anxiety, and he is unwilling or unable to change or seek professional help, it is time to let him go—at least until he has been certified normal again.

CHAPTER 20

❄

Beyond His Actions

If you are skeptical about committing to your man, there could be a good reason why—a reason that may have nothing to do with him playing games. It might be that there is something about his behavior that you're not quite comfortable with—and to make matters worse, you're not exactly sure what it is.

If you have been married for years, is there something about the way you communicate that you simple don't like, but you find it difficult to categorize and pinpoint? When you think it over, it's not about your love for him as much as it is about your negative feeling toward him that you have somehow developed. This feeling is based on negative thoughts that come and go, making you think it's all in your head. Or maybe you feel that you are affected by the way the media have aided in distorting your perception of black men in general. You are not even sure how much he has contributed to what you're feeling, if anything.

What adds to the dilemma is that you feel that he loves you. He expresses that love in his words and actions. In fact, all indications may even suggest that he has you on a pedestal.

After all, this is the same man who readily and gallantly defends your honor even with his own family members. You can recall the time his sister said that you were not a neat person. He didn't hesitate to go face to face with her to let her know how little he appreciated her comments. He even scorned his favorite aunt when she tried to talk about you negatively. Furthermore, to ensure that you are served properly in a restaurant, he will not hesitate to chew out a waiter.

Admittedly, you like it when your man makes a fuss over you—and why not? Still, it's not the attention paid you that's the problem. His actions might all be justifiable. However, it's his responses to the little things—the things that get you to looking beyond his actions to become fully conscious of how he reacts.

When a relationship is new and blossoming naturally, a man tends not to react to you too negatively—or at least not in the same way that he reacts to others. Thus, there is a tendency to overlook how he reacts or overreacts to life's challenges. But the way a black man consistently reacts to people and situations can be a valid clue to how he will eventually react to you. His style of reacting may also be the reason that you are experiencing feelings of apprehension in your relationship.

Because reactions happen less frequently than actions, they are sometimes more difficult to pinpoint as a problem area. Furthermore, a man may excuse some of his reactions on the ground that he was not thinking clearly and reacted too quickly.

However, consistently reacting unpredictably in a negative way is how some black men manage and control their relationships. A man who consistently reacts unpredictably in a negative way can keep you on edge trying to anticipate his reactions. At the same time, his behavior can keep you skeptical about the quality of your relationship. In some relationships, the way a man reacts can be so negative and unpredictable that a woman can find herself managing her life based on what she thinks his reactions will be.

Tracy was not fully aware that she was living in fear, trying to anticipate how Tony would "react" to the things she did. Surely, he loved her and some of his reactions were justifiable. Hence, it was difficult for her to clearly see how much stress his negative reactionary style of communication was causing her. Once she was aware that this was clearly a problem, Tracy documented a number of Tony's reactions before she said anything to him. As it turned out, he was not fully aware of his consistently negative reactionary behavior and the stress he was causing her as a result.

Make no mistake about it, everyone is capable of reacting unpredictably and negatively, even you. The problem arises when the tendency becomes a habit and a means to manage a relationship.

Quite often when a man makes a habit of reacting unpredictably in a negative way, he may cease striving to communicate clearly to you. Instead, he may start to depend on your ability to anticipate the things that he likes or doesn't like. A negative reaction can be anything from several days of silence to verbal or physical attacks.

Even if you are not living in fear, a man who uses this form of behavior as a means of communication can also bring unnecessary arguments to your relationship because of it.

The irony is that I believe most black men who use the unpredictability of their reactions as a method of control, management, and intimidation are doing so unconsciously. They don't say to themselves, "Today, I think I'll use negative reactions to communicate and control."

Even so, your wonderfully attentive black man can be very much in love with you and demonstrate it through his actions, while at the same time shifting your focus from feelings of love to feelings of anxiety and fear because of the way he reacts.

Should you find yourself in a relationship in which you can clearly see that his reaction to you is or could be a problem, you should nip it in the bud. As a recurring problem, it can become a menacing part of your relationship. Therefore, the sooner you talk about the issue, the better. Make sure that the first time you bring it up is not a time when he is in the act of reacting. Pick a quiet or loving time. Preface the conversation with something positive and uplifting, and then tell him. If it is an intricate part of the way he communicates, you should be prepared for him to react negatively to the discussion of how he reacts.

If you want to bring about change, you must be loving, respectful, and serious throughout the entire discussion. Let him know that his behavior is often a convenient way for him to be disrespectful, thereby avoiding real communication.

Some men may change after they become aware that they consistently react unpredictably in a negative way. If that is not what happens with your man, suggest alternative behavior to him. Suggest that rather than reacting, the two of you should gain a clear understanding of each other's expectations whenever possible. In addition, let him know that there will be times when the two of you simply will not have that clear understanding. Next, suggest that his first reaction should be to ask for clarification and understanding, and that you will try to do the same.

If at all possible, you both should avoid reacting negatively to a negative reaction. And finally, if this is a problem that you have identified but can't resolve, you are not alone—seek professional help.

PART FOUR

❄

The
Issues
We Face

CHAPTER 21

❄

You Make Mo Money

Yes! Black men are indeed threatened when black women make more money than they do. But they are threatened for more than the reasons that might come immediately to your mind—for example, it bruises their egos and questions their manhood.

When various black women confronted me with this issue, I was rather surprised. My initial thoughts were that this is an issue that black men rarely raise and discuss among themselves. Yet, black women are asking, "What's wrong with black men—why do they have a problem when we make more money?"

Indeed, one national survey showed that the vast majority of black men say they do not feel threatened dating a woman who has a larger income. When you think about it, why should he? The more money you make, the more money comes into the house. The solution is obviously not in you going to your source of income and insisting on a reduction in pay so that he can be happy.

Nevertheless, black men are threatened when black women make more money than they do. It's actually ludicrous for black couples to battle over such an issue as who makes more money.

Still, it's an issue that can have profound and sometimes devastating effects on black male-female relationships. Hopefully a discussion of the subject will increase your understanding and eliminate many unnecessary problems.

More and more black women are improving their economic situation. Unfortunately, they still carry around a lot of fairy-tale notions. One of these is that a smart, smiling, handsome prince with shiny black muscles will show up in his Mercedes and sweep them off their feet to happiness forever.

They hear a similar message in parent tales: "Honey, get yourself a doctor, a lawyer, a politician, or someone with a good career so you can live in a big house on Easy Street."

They hear it in girlfriend tales: "Girl, I prefer a movie star or some kind of entertainer. A brother that has it going on! You know what I mean."

They hear it when they tell themselves tales: "Although I'm going to do my own thing, I still want an ideal man, an athlete or someone making a lot of money. We will *both* have it going on."

What they hear are spoken and unspoken *dreams*. What they feel are the social pressures created for and often by black women. The dreams and the social pressures all too often imply that, if she can, a woman should marry into a life of money to find happiness (usually in that order). The pressures are often greater than you (or we as a people) would care to admit. But there is no need to bicker or cry about it. A woman marrying for her betterment is just fine. It's not a black or a white thing; nor am I implying that it is necessarily a bad thing.

Publicly, many black women scoff at the idea that they look for and only want to marry a man who has money. But others will insist that there is nothing wrong with it if they do.

A problem arises, however, when a woman, because of social conditioning, emphasizes the contents of a man's wallet rather than the contents of his character. With this fairy-tale emphasis, black women are feeling a need to have a good answer to the question, "What does he do for a living?"

But regardless of where black women stand on this issue, reality has wreaked havoc with the number of black men they have to choose from who measure up to the tales. Not only are black women faced with a shortage of black men who measure up, but they are faced with a shortage of black men in general.

The initial reaction of some black women to this shortage is to turn their backs on the fairy tale, claiming that they just want a man. Thus, many of them make the mistake of lowering their standards and failing to properly evaluate the men they communicate to. Then, after a few bad experiences, they start to say, "I no longer want just any man, I want a 'good' man."

Even so, from the media to friends and family members, black women are reminded of the fairy tales and the dreams of their ideal man. Then, if they find a good man, some black women begin to want him to measure up more closely to the standards of the tales. They start to feel that they settled for a less ideal man than they desired in the first place.

Some begin to resent their man because his job doesn't measure up to the dream. If they convince themselves that their position is reasonable, they may become condescending or belittling to the man. And if they have already given him what they feel is reasonable time to upgrade his employment status, their attitude may be even more caustic.

Women who have gone through such relationships feel justified when they blatantly ask a new man, "What kind of work do you do?" Or "Do you have a job?" Seemingly they might as well be saying, "I'm looking for the man of my dreams, and it's not so much his character I care about as his employment status."

They fail to realize that employment status is only one way to evaluate a black man—and a very limited one at that. A good job is often here today and gone tomorrow. If you are looking at his job as a primary criterion for desirability, you may end up with a "bad" man who has a "good" job. You would be better served to have a relationship with a positive and motivated black man who is underemployed or has no job than a well-employed man who is inherently negative.

Just as black women hear tales about finding a dream man, black men hear tales about *being* the dream man. Although they may be good at masking it, black men feel the pressure and the stress to live up to expectations defined by the tales. When you make more money than he does, it is a constant reminder that he isn't living up to the tales. The underlying message is that he is not your ideal man. Consequently, if he feels that he's inadequately employed, he might suffer from low self-esteem and insecurity.

There is little doubt that one of the main reasons that black men feel threatened when black women make more money than they do stems from their egos. But the primary reason that black men feel threatened by this stems from the black women's attitude and behavior.

Some of a man's attitude is likely to be based on what he thinks the public relationship that you and he have will be like when you make more money than he does. While you may or may not be concerned when people ask you what he does for a living, he may be secretly concerned about how it reflects on him that he is making less money than you.

Certainly, there is no excuse for the black man who has given up because he doesn't feel that he can get a job or get the "right" job. At the very least, he should be "creatively unemployed"—which means that he is actively working on bringing in an income. Yet, most black women know how difficult it can be for black men to get a good job.

Aside from the fact that there may be no jobs for what black men desire or are qualified for, the black male image, with its egotistical inclinations and its emphasis on manhood, causes some black men to have a problem with accepting jobs with wages and conditions that they consider below their subjective standards.

It's a problem that McDonald's acknowledges in its TV ad featuring Calvin, a young black man who starts out behind one of their cash registers. When his black male friends find out he's doing that kind of work, they imply through their behavior that it is below their standards and that they would rather do nothing than accept this kind of entry-level job. The ad goes on to show Calvin working his way up to management, and then implies that he will eventually own a franchise. The progression to management and ownership suggests to other young black men that working at McDonald's can meet their standards and fit with their understanding of the black male image.

Black men are aware that many jobs that are available to them are below their standards and do not fit black women's fairy-tale standards of the ideal man. Consequently, a number of black men choose unemployment over work that's looked down upon. They realize that with those jobs there is very little financial or psychological reward for them or their women.

Nevertheless, when a black woman is the only bread-winner in the house, she may view her mate's choice of unemployment as a negative option, feeling that he should take *some* work, even if it's not the ideal job for him. This is a predicament that often creates conflict in a black relationship.

One should not underestimate the influential power of the black male image here. There are some black men who would have a very difficult time taking work for work's sake. Some won't work at menial jobs unless they have absolutely no other option. Nevertheless, family obligation should always win out over individual voli-tion, even if this means that the man takes a job that is below his standards. A black man should perceive such work as a bridge to better things for him and his family, and not as his final stop in life.

It is with the vision of family in mind that black women should not hesitate to support black men, whether they are unemployed, underemployed, or a glowing success. Certainly, a man is expected to do this for a woman. As a people, we cannot afford anything less.

When black women have little or no patience for unemployed and underemployed black men, or when they belittle or ignore black men who have less than ideal work, they miss the vital importance of black family, companionship, and love.

Still, things like loneliness and being alone during holidays and social functions will sometimes serve to remind certain black women of the importance of a good relationship, even when their man is not gainfully employed.

Many relationships come down to what a black woman can do to motivate her man to follow his dream, keep looking for work after he's been rejected many times, or accept work that he considers below his standards. He might more easily accomplish the latter task if he is assured that you are not influenced by outside pressures and are not secretly resentful because he is not the ideal financial man or the man that tales are made of.

When Herb got out of the military, neither he nor Lola thought that two long years would pass without him finding employment. Although he had supported the family during the six years he was in the military, she had made it known to all who would listen that she was tired of supporting the family now. After two years, Herb felt he needed a good job to make up for the lost wages. At the same time, he was losing his motivation to diligently seek employment. Lola was demonstrating less and less respect for him, while publicly maintaining that it was time for him to get work, regardless of how low the wages were. This situation was taking its toll on their relationship. Herb began to respond as many black men have done in this situation. He started feeling desperate and wanted to shirk his responsibility altogether. At a time when Herb and Lola most needed to pull together, they were starting to lose sight of family strength and unity, and thus were falling apart.

There is no image more diametrically opposed to the black man's image or the black woman's image of the ideal man than that of a man as a homemaker. But we are at a time when the sooner black couples accept house husbandry as a realistic and viable option, the better. Whether the situation is viewed as transitional or permanent, both parties need to come to terms with it.

This brings me back to the primary reason why black men are often intimidated when black women make as much money as they do, or more. It has everything to do with the attitude and behavior of black women when they are in the breadwinning position. Consciously and unconsciously, they can be and often are more assertive and confrontational. At times they are less tolerant. The breadwinning black woman might even subscribe to the golden rule theory, believing that "the one who makes the gold makes the rules."

In this situation, the black man who is either unemployed or underemployed, or who is a homemaker, is put in check or controlled by his woman. He feels disconnected from the important authoritative aspect of the black male image, and therefore he loses contact with a part of his manhood. He is very likely to show insecure behavior when he has to disconnect from the black male image involuntarily. He might demonstrate behavior that he never demonstrated before—behavior that implies a weak rather than a strong man. For example, he might become overly concerned that his woman will be unfaithful, or that he might lose her altogether. It's a predicament that often leaves incurable wounds to his ego and subsequently to your relationship.

On the other hand, black women often have the power to change and save a relationship that's in transition. But what happens, far too often, is that other family members, acquaintances, and blacks in general will frown on a situation in which the woman is working and the man is not. It reminds them of the days (the 1970s) when black men made it their business to pimp and use black women. Although there are black men who still demonstrate that behavior, we must nevertheless attempt to heal ourselves and move forward, realizing that without each other African Americans will never maximize their potential. Put out something positive and let it flow. When you help somebody, it will eventually come back to you.

This doesn't mean that you should let a man have his way to the extent that he can take advantage of you. It does mean, however, that you have mutual respect and that you want to uplift the man in your life. Those outside influences will cause you to second-guess yourself and question his motives. After all, suppose you give him all this support and he gets on his feet and leaves you. But that's not likely to happen if you stick with what's in this book. Nevertheless, blacks should always seek to uplift each other, regardless of the nature of their relationship. We can't afford any more crabs in the barrel. As a whole, we need to be more concerned about uplifting each other than about someone getting over on us if we help them.

Perhaps you have a situation in which your man is not exactly loving his predicament or showing the greatest self-esteem or appreciation of you. Meanwhile, you're getting negative input from friends and family that he's getting over on you. The combined chemistry could make for a volatile and ugly relationship. Remember, this is all because you have a job and he doesn't.

I must emphasize that the entire question of who's making more money is really a non-issue, particularly when you take a look at the big picture, which includes the economic status of blacks in general. Again, in many cases, it's not so much the amount of money you make as the change in your attitude that intimidates black men. Even when you don't think that you have changed, be mindful of subtle differences in your behavior.

If you think that your man has a problem with you making more money than he does, and if family life is important to you, take control. Go out of your way to convince him that it is his character and not his wallet that's most important. In the words of Arlene, who made considerably more money than her husband Dave, "He knows I make more money, but he also knows that he's the man of this house."

If your man does not feel that way, don't hesitate to ensure that he does. If you have told him before and he is still insecure, tell him again. Tell him with your words and let your actions back you up. It's not the quantity but the quality of your statements that does the convincing. The quality will be right when he is convinced that your love for him genuinely exceeds the love you have for the money he makes. Surely, at that moment, the black man in your life will no longer be intimidated by you making more money than he does.

CHAPTER 22

❄

Watch Out

Stay cautiously alert! There may be a woman intruding in your life who has ruined many relationships. Demanding and dazzling as she can be, this woman has the unsavory nerve to shamelessly invite herself into your home and particularly your bedroom. Unknowingly, you will lead her right to your man, then watch as she purposefully engages his attention. Not only is she calculating; quite often she appears physically beautiful to him, particularly when she has little or nothing on. As if that's not insulting enough, she attempts to take him places you haven't even dreamed of going. Usually she's what he wants her to be. She's often witty, sensuous, and knowledgeable, seldom has a weight problem, and seems forever young.

But she's not *that* perfect. She gives him fallible advice on who he is and what he can be and should be in life. If you are not watchful, she will cater to him enough to make him lazy and comfortable in his laziness. She will even have you thinking that she's your friend, and you might turn to her for comfort yourself. With her attention-getters, she will eventually affect the quality of communication between the two of you and thus the quality of your relationship.

This unsuspiciously yet powerfully addicting person is none other than your television set! Now, you might shrug your shoulders or breathe a sigh of relief, but maybe you shouldn't. There's a good chance that you have at least one TV set in your home, and probably more.

Television, the "other woman," is often an unexamined or forgotten factor that helps to erode the quality of black male-female relationships, and you should beware! No other group of people in America watch as much television as we do. You are watching blindly if you can't see that it will have an effect on your relationship and your family.

In a new relationship, television is often used to help break the ice, to smooth over those silent moments when you are searching for the right things to say and discuss. But then it finds a nice snug place in-between you and your man. Over time, not only does it smooth over silent moments between you and your mate, but it starts to create them. Gradually it will increase its role in your relationship. Thus, it's often a mistake to establish a relationship in which it is the center of attention. Time can pass and you'll think you're getting to know each other, when in fact what you are really getting to know is what the other person likes to watch.

People who communicate and know each other primarily through their TV watching don't really know each other very well, if at all. Television can be too great a distraction to facilitate the kind of one-on-one communication that leads to quality love and understanding between two people.

If your television set were really "another woman," you would accuse her right off the bat of trying to take your man. You would be royally upset and concerned during those times when he listens to and watches her and not you. You would be keenly aware of how much she robs you of your time alone and of how often she determines what you discuss. You might even become aware that she's the source of little arguments over such things as what to watch, when to watch it, and how loud she should be.

Ultimately you might even discover that you have developed a language to better accommodate her presence: sign language and facial expressions that say, "Don't interrupt during this program or while she is speaking" or "Talk softly so that she can be heard." You end up giving each other half your attention and her the other half. Your affection often amounts to TV first, humans second. Yet, because it is a television set and not a woman, you can easily fall under the illusion that the three of you are getting along just fine.

Look, I like to watch television, and I realize it can be difficult to leave it alone. Let's face it, TV can be very entertaining. But let's face some other realities, too. TV is a path of least resistance that can lower you into a lazy hypnotic state. Researchers say it takes less energy to watch TV than it does to chew gum. It certainly takes willpower to turn the set off. And again, African Americans are watching more of it than any other ethnic group in the nation. No doubt it is affecting our relationships, both with our mates and our children, and we must address it.

If you are starting a new relationship, you would do well to build your foundation taking into account the negative influence that television watching can have. Then you can plan accordingly and lessen its impact on your relationship.

On the other hand, if your man is an avid television watcher or maybe even an addict, you will discover that it's not that easy to pull him away. It won't take long for you to see just how much television has already come between you.

In fact, you are likely to meet stiff resistance. Any antagonistic move on your part may quickly escalate the situation into a heated argument. Resist the temptation to confront him until you devise a plan and have the patience to discuss it. That way you will have a much greater impact.

First, attempt to get him to agree that since blacks watch more television than any other group, we all need to watch less.

Then estimate how much of a reduction in television

watching would be a reasonable goal in your relationship. Let's use 25 percent as an example:

(1) To accomplish that goal, you might get rid of all your television sets except one.

(2) If you have a TV in your bedroom, it should be the first to go. Then rediscover each other all over again, and/or get more sleep.

(3) Invest in a TV guide each week. As a rule of thumb, never watch without first consulting it.

(4) Go through your TV guide, highlight everything you would normally watch, and then decide what to cut out. Avoid watching rerun programs that you have already seen.

(5) Highlight everything you watch during a normal week. After one month, go over your highlighted TV guides and see how much time you spend with the set on. Then cut back 25 percent.

(6) Decide on how many hours a day it would take to meet your goal, and try to limit your viewing to that time.

(7) Acknowledge that initially you may not appear to be as entertaining as the television programs.

(8) Prepare in advance some things you can do or talk about that can enhance your quality of time together.

(9) Work on developing more common interests. For example, you could read and discuss one book a month that the two of you agree upon.

(10) Never turn on the TV for background noise.

(11) Acknowledge that it may not be easy to follow

your plan, and sometimes you may slip. But stay on track anyway.

(12) Reward yourself for your success as you progress.

CHAPTER 23

❄

Black Men/White Women

Consider the struggle that black men have had to come to grips with in understanding the boundaries of their own sexuality. Add to that a desire to date and marry white women, and you have one of the most talked about, denounced, taboo, and misunderstood relationship issues around.

Although "jungle fever" is an increasingly used term to describe the condition of black men who date or desire white women, it does not explain why they have it.

What I call the "white cycle" has a great deal to do with explaining why black men pursue and date white women. It may also shed some light on why some black women charge black men with being white-woman crazy.

Granted, more enlightenment may not stop some black women from having feelings of betrayal or frustration when they see a black man with a white woman, but it may help to considerably reduce those inevitable emotions.

Furthermore, if you are rearing a black male, understanding the "white cycle" may help you to bring a better balance to his developing thoughts and perceptions of white women. To achieve that balance is certainly an opportunity that black women should seize, but gently, firmly, and effectively. From your input, he should be able to clearly surmise that there is no premium or added value to the white woman's sexuality because of her skin color.

In effect, it is the premium given to the white female's sexuality by society in general that angers many black women when they see a black man with a white woman. Implied in the premium is that because of skin color, white women are more valuable or better than black women. That may be one underlying reason why some black women are more bothered by seeing a black man with a white woman than with a woman of any other race. They resent the premium given to the white woman's sexuality and thus her skin color. Black women are highly aware of how ridiculous the premium is, but they are not confident that black men share their understanding. This is especially true when they see a black man walking more proudly with a white woman than they think he would walk with a black woman.

Therefore, when a single black woman sees a black man with a white woman, she is likely to receive two negative messages. One says, "He is not available for me or my single black female friends during this black male shortage." The other says, "He thinks he has something more with her"—which implies that a black woman is something less.

In facing this issue, we all know that the premium does not exist, except maybe psychologically—and then only to an extent that I will explain later.

First, I must point out that most people, both black and white, admit that when they see a black man with a white woman they are inclined to believe that the two came together because of their sexual desires. I interpret this to mean that these people are aware of how society in general has exalted both the black man's and the white woman's sexuality.

Moreover, it is precisely because of the exaltation and exploitation of black men's sexuality that many of them go through the "white cycle." This is the process they go through when they rid themselves of the psychological influence of society's exaltation of the white woman's sexuality. Secondarily, it involves ridding themselves of the psychological influence of society's exaltation of their own sexuality. The "white cycle" is by no means an excuse for black men who cross racial lines, nor is it intended to be. Nevertheless, the "white cycle" exists, and black men go through it.

The "white cycle" begins when black men start to believe that there is a premium or added value to the white woman's sexuality simply because she is white. Furthermore, many start to believe that they must find out if it's true, either from hearsay or, more commonly, from their own experience. In any event, the belief itself starts the cycle, while lingering fascination often strengthens their desire and lures them to its core.

On the one hand, black men are deluged with images and messages that often imply, sometimes blatantly, that white women are the epitome of female sexuality. The underlying message about white women's sexuality appears in newspapers, magazines, television programs, films, and all the other media. The movie *Indecent Proposal* set a white woman's sexual value at one million dollars for one night. Black men also get the message about the added premium of white women's sexuality from the women themselves, many of whom go out of their way to prove, through their mannerisms and behavior, that there is indeed added value to them because of their skin color. For example, if a black man looks at a white woman or shows interest in her, she is likely to react as if he is doing this because she is white, and any other reason is secondary.

On the other hand, there is very little done to stop or counter the continuous media bombardment of the black man's mind with images hyping the sexuality of the white woman. Yet, it is either implied or stated that he can't have her, or that she's forbidden—which often only serves to enhance his desire for her as well as his belief that she has added value.

One should not underestimate the accumulative effect that the images and messages about the white woman's sexuality can and do have on black men. Most of them have already learned from society and/or the black male sexual image that expressing themselves sexually is a way of demonstrating their manhood. Moreover, the more a black man expresses his sexuality, the more man he thinks he is. In several of our most integrated cities, a majority of black men under the age of forty-four admit that they either had sex or desired to have sex with white women. This no doubt has a great deal to do with the way society has exalted the sexuality of white women.

Hence, many a black man expects a white woman's skin color to make a difference in what he would experience with her sexually. Not surprisingly, some black men candidly admit that they feel that their sexual experience with white women is or was enhanced because the women are white. These men don't realize how the psychological influence of society's exaltation of the white woman has distorted their own perceptions of her.

For the vast majority of black men, however, one or a few encounters will bring them to reality and out of the "white cycle." They then clearly realize that a woman's skin color does not enhance the sexual experience. Those black men who have a problem breaking out of the "white cycle" usually have the problem because they are overwhelmed by the continuous bombardment of messages exalting the sexuality of the white woman. Black women's resentment and anger, along with society's pressures, are obviously not enough to overcome the impact of that bombardment. In fact, this resentment, anger, and pressure may very well make a black man think that there must be something real to the allure of the white woman.

I was at a networking function in which there were nearly one hundred black women present. Many were very attractive. I was asking various people relationship questions. At one point, I asked a black man if he was interested in any of the women there. He shamelessly confided in me that he had his eye on one of the two white women present. Here was a black man in the midst of many beautiful black women, and yet he was trapped in the "white cycle."

While struggling with the "white cycle" problem, many black men will go into denial because it's much too shameful to admit that they have "jungle fever" and need to get through the "white cycle" to get rid of it. Moreover, when a black man does admit that he has the problem, many people, particularly black women, are inclined to call him white-woman crazy, as if that would cure him. Clearly, these women are overlooking the fact that their own brothers or sons can easily get caught in the "white cycle."

But as I mentioned earlier, the "premium" does not exist except psychologically. Many people would argue that if it exists psychologically, then it exists, period. But in reality, each experience that a black man has with a white woman can potentially and will eventually show him that there is no premium. Thus, reality often serves as the cure.

Sometimes, however, nothing less than therapy will help end the "white cycle." Black therapists and psychologists should identify the "white cycle" problem and address it.

Additionally, it would behoove black men to become more conscious of the societal influences that exalt the white woman, and they should candidly discuss among themselves the impact of these influences.

For their part, many white women expect something more from the sexuality of black men, just as many black men expect something more from them. Even so, because black men grow up learning to believe in the power of their penises, sexual enhancement for their partners is the one thing most black men believe they can deliver. Some believe it enough that they feel an experience with them can make a white woman desire them, or black men in general, for the rest of her life. This is in part the origin for the saying, "Once you go black, you never go back." In some cases, black men and white women have such high expectations of each other that the experience itself could never live up to the fantasy.

The "white cycle" ends when those black men who have been psychologically affected by the aggrandizement of the white woman's skin color clearly realize that they can have a good or bad experience with *any* woman, and that skin color in and of itself has no added value.

It must be pointed out, however, that not all black-white relationships are a by-product of the "white cycle."

Furthermore, once a black man has gone through it, he might still become attracted to a white woman, but for reasons other than those induced by the "white cycle."

It must also be pointed out that there are many black men who have no desire to experience sex with white women simply because they are white. Many of these men have a realistic understanding of their own and white women's sexuality. One way or another, they have managed to escape the influence of the hype.

We can no longer ignore the hype and then despise its results. Young black males have to be taught that this society exalts the white woman's sexuality, either inadvertently or purposely, and that this ultimately will have them believing that she is more valuable because of her skin color. At the same time, they have to be taught that the hype is telling them that their mothers and other black women are less valuable because of their skin color. Moreover, it is not enough to simply make them aware of media exploitation in general. Specific examples are plentiful and should occasionally be pointed out.

The idea is not to frustrate young black males or make them angry. Nor is it to pass on deep feelings of resentment that you might have. Rather, it is to educate them and lay the proper foundation for healthy perceptions. If *you* don't do it, who will? With your teachings, black males can avoid the "white cycle." Then, should a black male you have taught choose to date a white woman, it would be because of her character and not her skin color.

Thus, you and no other black women will ever see him acting as if he has something better because the woman with him is white.

Black women will sometimes ask black men if they have dated or are currently dating white women. Some ask because they appreciate and often prefer black men who don't date white women. If they find themselves with a black man who dated white women in the past, they are guardedly hoping that he has completed the "white cycle."

One might ask, "Regardless of how black men got there, doesn't the 'white cycle' confirm that many of them are white-woman crazy?" The answer is no. Black men are not white-woman crazy, as many people would have you believe. If the term has any meaning at all, it would be more accurate to say that black men can be women-crazy, and white women are simply an extension of that. Given the way that many black men have been acclimated to their sexuality, a woman to them is a woman, and skin color just happens to be one more influencing factor—albeit sometimes a strong one.

Some black women are quick to point out that they believe black men prefer white women. But don't believe the hype. Much of what these women believe stems from seeing black men who are trapped in the "white cycle." Black men want sexual experiences. It's no secret that these desires often include white women. I explained earlier that sex is what the men want—but it is not what they are looking for.

Furthermore, in asserting that some black men seem to have an insatiable desire for white women, some black women maintain that the proof can be found in black men who proudly date physically unattractive white women just because they are white. That might indeed be true. Aside from the fact that beauty is in the eye of the beholder, sometimes his choice is due to his limited access to white women.

However, the elevation of the white woman's sexuality in general is sometimes so strong that the psychological influence allows her skin color to blunt a black man's criticism of any of her other physical attributes—in some cases, long enough for him to complete the "white cycle."

The question of whether or not white women are a serious threat to black women will always depend on one's perspective. Even though 98 percent of all black men date and marry black women, to many black women one black man with a white woman is threat enough.

Naturally, a relationship has many more elements than elevated sexual attraction. As the novelty of having access to white women dissipates, along with the psychological impact of the "white cycle," choosing white women because of their skin color will no longer become the short-term or long-term choice of black men.

Even now, the majority of those black men who go through the "white cycle" return to black women, sometimes with increased desire. Statistics strongly support the fact that most black men who have dated white women still prefer black women.

Nevertheless, despite everything said here, you still may not empathize with a black man going through the "white cycle." You may not welcome him with open arms when he returns, but at least you'll know the deal.

CHAPTER 24

❄

One Way Out

Love is what you're giving him. Contempt is what you're getting back. What was once pure love is now icy, painful, and burdensome. Your heart is in the right place, but it seems that nothing else is.

You hate to let him go because you have invested so much time. Besides, the type of love you have runs deep. It's solid commitment. Yet, he has the audacity to be mentally and verbally abusive. Sometimes you think you want out, but the problem lies in your heart. You feel you're trapped by a thing called love.

This book is about getting and keeping love, marriage, and commitment forever. If you take heed to the information that's here, I believe that you should be able to get them. I also realize that there comes a time when you are faced with the idea of having to let go, particularly when you are not yet married. Maybe you only have a sexship, and perhaps you really don't believe he can be faithful; yet you hold on. You are faced with realizing that you are in a mismatched relationship, and that the man you love is simply not for you.

Perhaps you know he has another woman, and he seems to be far more in love with her than he is with you. But you read somewhere that love was never meant to be rational. So you keep giving and giving because you think love is making you do it. But when you think about it, it's jealousy of the other woman that keeps you chasing. Certainly, it's nothing he has consistently done in recent memory. You're giving love and you really want love back. As Teddy Pendergrass said, "It's so good to love somebody when that somebody loves you back."

In reality, the man is rejecting you, and you don't want to face it. We all get our share of being rejected, if that's any consolation. Ironically, there is a tendency to fall deeper into the love pit during rejection—just when one should be climbing out.

Well, it's time to stop feeling sorry for yourself. This cycle you are going through is quite typical. It's what happens when you love a black man too much. You are busting 10 on the Love Scale, and he's down at 2. Furthermore, he knows you will do almost anything for him regardless of the consequences, because you have already proven that.

Now let's fast-forward and say that you have been practicing what's in this book, and he's *still* not acting right. I would say that either he has a real problem or the two of you are just incompatible. Maybe you're waiting for him to say the words, "It's over." Many women like to hear "The End" said in words. If you're one of them, you should be aware that many black men tell you it's over with their actions long before they say it with their mouths—if they ever say it at all. Some don't say it verbally because they know you will keep holding on. Plus, it keeps the door open for them to take advantage of you if they desire. Quite often, when a man does finally say it verbally, it's because you have already been *totally* replaced by another woman.

Okay, stay with me now. I promise to show you one way out. But first, let's take a look at what typically happens to the heart while you're waiting for the words "It's over."

Many black women will set themselves up not just to have their hearts broken, but to have their self-esteem shattered, during the time that the relationship is over but they're waiting for the man to say it. As he continues to distance himself, the woman starts to doubt her ability to maintain a solid relationship. What she is sure about is that she gave so much of herself, and it was all in vain.

Among those women who stay in negative relationships too long, some find it tough to recover. When they do manage to pull their life back together, they have hardened their hearts. Many grow bitter toward black men in general, particularly if this kind of thing happens to them more than once. While some take on a seriously negative attitude, others proclaim that they now will only date white men because black men ain't…this or that.

Believe it or not, one of the best things you can do is

to mend your heart *before* you leave the relationship. To do so means to exit out of strength, with your self-esteem, dignity, and heart intact.

You must come to realize that we experience each other through our thoughts. No matter how much you love, hate, or mentally hurt, the only way you can have that experience is through your thoughts. It doesn't matter how good or bad a person makes you feel. That is why two people can go through the same experience and have a different perception of it. The only way you can get to that experience is through your thoughts. It follows that the only way you can love a man too much is through your thoughts. So change your thoughts and you will change your feelings.

You say that's not that easy? Of course it is. Change that thought, too!

The goal is to remove yourself from the relationship mentally before you do it physically. Men do it all the time. If you have a change of heart, and you and he start over, mentally come back slowly and cautiously. Monitor your relationship and take nothing for granted.

But for now, find some time when you are alone and visualize the relationship being over. Think about life after him. And, believe me, there *is* life after him. But go ahead and think about the worst-case scenario. Go through it in your mind and feel the pain, the loneliness, the heartbreak, and all that they entail. Experience the emotions and let them out. Cry if you want to. Then, when you have finished this exercise, go have yourself a good cup of herb tea or your favorite juice.

Next, start to concentrate your thoughts on his negative characteristics or what you don't like about him. If you focus on enough negatives, or one prominent negative, you will begin to affect the thoughts you have about your love for him. Use those thoughts to decrease your love and come down on the Love Scale. You will know this is working when you try the first exercise again and it doesn't hurt nearly as much, if at all. You will have gotten mentally stronger!

This exercise could possibly save your relationship. If you love him too much, you know by now that that is a serious part of the problem. But if he's not giving you the love you feel you deserve, you can't be all that happy. And more than likely, things will get worse before they get better. Therefore, concentrate on those things that you don't like about him. He's not that perfect! After all, he can't see the beauty in having you as his woman.

When at last you have sufficiently decreased your love for him, you will have the heart, nerve, and power it takes to bring balance to your relationship, or you will have the strength it takes to walk away. Very often, when you're at this point, it is that very strength that will bring him back to you with new love and respect—*if* you decide you still want him.

If you need additional punch, break up with him first. You can do it verbally because you have already done it mentally. Be prepared to let him go. This can rattle his black male image enough to make him want you back. Also remember, no man is going to want to be with a sad and negative woman, particularly one he has already lost interest in. Therefore, it's also imperative that you assume a positive upbeat attitude as soon as possible throughout this process. The mental exercise described above should help you in that area as well. Be positive, calm, and confident around him and the people he knows. If there is any chance of the relationship working, you have positioned yourself to receive him back or confidently move on.

Conclusion

Your destiny is now firmly on the path to a very successful relationship. You can be confident that you know why black men commit forever. Certainly, you now know that although they may very passionately "want" sex, it is not what they are looking for, and they will not commit because of it—even if they think it's great.

The information in this book has given you an absolute psychological edge. Use it to enhance your relationship—and ultimately the family.

Don't let past mistakes deflate your self-esteem or hinder you in any way. Never again shall you reach for the security of love and be left hanging on to empty promises.

From now on, be the ruler of your man's heart. Wisely monitor your relationship to ensure love and commitment. Don't hesitate to balance your love with his on the Love Scale. Or even let the Scale lean to your advantage and then confidently open your heart as he falls deeper in love with you.

You can and should forever enjoy a relationship in which thoughts of you stay on your man's mind—a relationship in which he can't get enough of your love because you have a Claire Huxtable Attitude and have used femininity to its maximum. Also, use common interests to bond with your man. Then you'll see his actions saying, "I have a thing for you, and I can't let go!"

Furthermore, you are now keenly aware that there are good men with bad games, just as there are unscrupulous men with bad games. You can recognize and stay several steps ahead of the games, or stop them altogether.

The man in your life will commit to you forever. Whether your GEM (Good Ebony Man) is an obvious asset or a diamond in the rough, establish a friendship based on respect and love, then confidently seek and insist on commitment. It's commitment and not love that keeps relationships together. People who love each other often walk away and rely on divorce as a solution. But people who are committed do not.

Moreover, be committed to realizing your own value. Certainly, you are more precious to black men than they could ever put in words—or maybe even want you to know. You nurture them! You love them! You help them to mature! You empower them! Make no mistake about it—you are invaluable to them!

While I have equipped you to properly address issues concerning your mate, the ultimate answer to problems in relationships lies in knowing that you should keep God as a focal point. Then, when you are faced with a problem, you can be guided by His wisdom. This does not mean that you neglect your problems. It simply means that you don't dwell on them.

If you and your GEM get to the point where you focus on God through your thoughts and prayer life, it is then that you will truly have all it takes to maintain a relationship filled with love, happiness, and commitment forever. May you be the recipient of God's blessings!

# copies	Title	Price	S&H	Total
____	*Black Men Not Looking for Sex:* *Why They Commit Forever*	$12.95	+ $2 =	$14.95
____	*The Cold Reality:* *How to Get and Keep a Black* *Man in a Relationship*	$9.95	+ $2 =	$11.95
____	*How to Have a Super Relationship* *Anytime! Anywhere!*	$5.00	+ $2 =	$7.00

Total _____

California residents add 7.75% tax

— —

Name _____

Address _____

City _____ State_____ Zip _____

Send to: Zevon Publications
           P.O. Box 4764-B
           San Jose, CA 95150

Thank you for your order!